A Spiritual Journey
WHY I BECAME A CHRISTIAN SCIENTIST

•

Richard A. Nenneman

Also by Richard A. Nenneman

The New Birth of Christianity:
Why Religion Persists In A Scientific Age

Persistent Pilgrim:
The Life of Mary Baker Eddy

A Spiritual Journey
WHY I BECAME A CHRISTIAN SCIENTIST

•

Richard A. Nenneman

Nebbadoon Press

A Spiritual Journey: Why I Became A Christian Scientist

©2008 Richard A. Nenneman Irrevocable Trust

All rights preserved. Printed in the Untied States of America. No part of this book may be used of reproduced in any manner whatsoever without written permission except in the case of brief quotations embodied in critical articles and reviews.

For information, contact the Publisher:

Nebbadoon Press
800 500-9086
Contact@NebbadoonPress.com

ISBN 1-891331-04-3

Contents

PART ONE

Preface *1*

Chapter 1 My Religious Background; Importance Of Religion; Early Interest In Christian Science *5*

Chapter 2 Ralph Waldo Emerson *17*

Chapter 3 Thoughts About God and Jesus in the Middle Ages *27*

Chapter 4 A Concept of God for Today *35*

Chapter 5 Eschatology—The Meaning of Jesus *45*

Chapter 6 The Hebrew Scriptures *71*

Chapter 7 William James *83*

Chapter 8 Dietrich Bonhoeffer *91*

Chapter 9 Relating to Other Religions *101*

Chapter 10 Church as Community *113*

Chapter 11 The Christian Science Church *117*

Chapter 12 Finding Your Own Way *129*

PART TWO

Autobiography 1929 – 2007 *139*

An Appreciation by David Cook *245*

Bibliography *249*

Dedicated to my grandchildren

Mark Robson
Jeremy Robson
Katherine Wrean
William Wrean
Ashley Wrean

In Memoriam:
Craig Roberts
Joshua Roberts

ACKNOWLEDGEMENTS

It is with much gratitude and admiration that I thank Jane and George Spitzer of Nebbadoon Press for their diligence and patience in producing this book. The work of editing and making transitions from separate manuscripts to make a coherent book is very well done and was necessary as my husband had not completed the book before his death.

Thanks go to Harry Hoehler and my daughters for compiling the manuscripts, editing, and checking sources.

A paragraph from "Letters and Papers from Prison" by Dietrich Bonhoeffer epitomizes my concept of the life Dick and I spent together:

"Most people have forgotten nowadays what a home can mean, though some of us have come to realize it as never before. It is a kingdom of its own in the midst of the world, a stronghold amid life's storms and stresses, a refuge, even a sanctuary. It is not founded on the shifting sands of outward or public life, but it has its peace in God, for it is God who gives it its special meaning and value, its own nature and privilege, its own destiny and dignity. It is an ordinance of God in the world, the place in which—whatever may happen in the world—peace, quietness, joy, love, purity, discipline, respect, obedience, tradition, and, with it all, happiness may dwell."

Katherine L. Nenneman
May 2008

PART ONE

PREFACE

I became motivated to write what follows by wondering just what two of my grandchildren are learning in Sunday School each week. Do the discussions they have instill in them a keen sense of ethical conduct? Does it make them begin to think about what the word "God" means in their own lives? Do the discussions in Sunday School have a direct connection with how they acted—and reacted—to the events in their lives during the following week?

Then my thoughts went back to my own Sunday School days, first as a preteenager in what I would call a moderately evangelical Protestant church, and later for almost a year in a Christian Science Sunday School. I realized that between my preteen years and the last year of my teens I had made a remarkable spiritual journey. We do not always make that journey in our teens. And for many of us, the concerns of religion do not seem to count for much until later in life. We are too busy maturing both physically and mentally. As young adults, getting started with a career and at some point finding a life companion preoccupy us. It may be only when we are thirty or forty that we discover the importance of a spiritual link in our lives that can make a major difference in all that we set out to do.

So, although I began writing this as a rather long letter to my grandchildren, I realized when I had finished it that it might not have meaning for them for several more decades. With that in mind, I have tried to describe my own religious pilgrimage in terms that may be helpful to those of any age. And it *is* a pilgrimage. Although I am a student of Christian Science, my own vision, or understanding, of spiritual reality continues to evolve.

In the first two chapters I explain the important influence of my religious parents and the writings of Ralph Waldo Emerson. Then, after the four sections dealing with concepts of God, Jesus, and something about the significance of the Hebrew Scriptures, I jump to modern times and another American philosopher, William James, who came at the end of the nineteenth century. James has been important to me for at least three reasons. First, like Emerson, his style is engaging. This is most easily recognized in *The Varieties of Religious Experience*. There is an old canard that claims James wrote philosophy like a novelist, while his brother Henry, the novelist, wrote novels like a philosopher. The *Varieties* tells of religious experience in terms of real people. Second, and more important, James recognized the validity of some forms of spiritual healing. At the very least, he recognized the ability of religious faith to revitalize lives. Finally, I am impressed by his regard for his own conviction and the courage to act on conviction.

This is what led me to include a chapter on the German theologian, Dietrich Bonhoeffer. Of course one could choose a myriad of individuals who have given their all, as he did, for their convictions. But my generation grew up during the Nazi period and World War II. Those years have formed the background to our entire adult lives to this day, and trying to understand how a civilized country like Germany was even partially seduced by Hitler has always intrigued me. So the story of Bonhoeffer finds its way into the otherwise very American approach to religion. He was a man, as I say, of whom James would have been proud.

The final four chapters all seemed necessary to me because of the times in which we live. Relating to other religions would not have been a serious topic for most people a century, or even two generations, ago. Today, instead of having come through a century that would make all the world the "Christian Century," as the magazine was called, we have entered a multipolar religious world. It is not the diabolical misuses to which some Muslims have put their own religion that concerns me here. Rather, there is a need for genuine appreciation for the faiths that have nurtured and continue to nurture the lives of millions of their adherents, as well as a need to think about how we relate this appreciation to our own religious beliefs and practice.

I address the issue of whether one can develop a spiritual life alone. There are huge differences among church congregations in the United States today. They range from megachurches with several thousand members to small groups of ten or fifteen. Even when we acknowledge the need to meet as people engaged on a similar journey, the ways in which we do that can be vastly different. Church needs to be mutually supportive, and at its best, it is. But it is also on occasion divisive or competitive, which is why there are individuals who prefer to get their church on television or not participate at all.

Finally, how can one progress in developing a sense of God's presence, which to me is what religion is all about? In the case of Christian Science in particular, in which one's convictions demand action, demand some kind of practice that follows on the conviction, where can one find help and encouragement in a society that, at least on a superficial level, is overwhelmingly secular, hedonistic, and materialistic?

If the spiritual life is actually the primary demand on us, as I believe it is, what kind of practices can we follow that will help us promote its attainment?

Chapter One

MY RELIGIOUS BACKGROUND; IMPORTANCE OF RELIGION; EARLY INTEREST IN CHRISTIAN SCIENCE

When I see my grandchildren, Mark and Jeremy playing outside our Sunday School on a Sunday morning, waiting for their parents to take them to the day's next event—a soccer, basketball, or baseball game, depending on the season of the year—I often think back to the days when I was a Sunday School pupil in Chicago. There were no organized school teams in those days, at least not for grade-school kids. There was also almost nothing that could be called "organized" on Sunday with the exception of church activities. There was not even any TV to go home to watch. This was in the late 1930s, just before World War II.

The rest of Sunday in our house was a very quiet day. My Lutheran aunt, who lived in Louisville, said she always hated Sundays because nothing happened. At our house, my mother, who was more openly religious than my dad, might play some of the old hymns she liked and take a nap. My father would work in his garden or take a walk or read. Like my aunt, I did not particularly like Sundays because, as she said, nothing ever happened.

But one thing was certain. This was a day apart. And if it did not make you "religious," it did serve the purpose of making you believe that religion is a very important part of your life. So I am glad when I see you at Sunday School. At the same time, there are so many things I would like to tell you about what my religious experience has been that I am going to try to write it down for you. It may not seem as important right now, or even when you are at college. But somewhere along the way I hope you recognize that the role religion has played in our lives for centuries is, or at least should continue to be, one of most vital elements of your own life. In some ways, it is the thing that ties together everything else we do.

Before I get into that, though, I have to mention some of the hymns that we sang with some regularity in our church. This was an interdenominational church in a suburban part of Chicago. We had a Presbyterian minister. I do not know whose hymnal we used, but many of the hymns would be familiar to most Protestants. The one we sang the most was "Holy, Holy, Holy," to the point where I cannot bear to look at it even today in the Christian Science Hymnal. Two more were "Come Thou Almighty King" and "The Church's One Foundation"—both referring to Jesus, of course. A bit more on the sentimental side was "Safely Through Another Week." It goes on to say "God has brought us on our way."

I knew, even if I could not put it into words at the time, that God was not a "big person" looking out for me or judging me, but how does one conceive of the idea of God other than as person? At least that would have been my answer in those days. Many of the hymns certainly gave one the impression that God was waiting to hear from us—hymns such as "Be not dismayed what e'er betide, God will take care of you." And then there were those that seemed to mix the name of God with Jesus, so I wasn't sure whom they were talking about—such as "What a Friend We have in Jesus," in which one line says what awful grief we bear, "all because we do not take it to the Lord in prayer." These were powerful thoughts: The fact that more than sixty years later I can remember many of them word for word attests to the impression they made at the time.

My independent thoughts about religious belief did not really begin until I was in high school. In 1941, I joined the church I have just talked about, at the age of twelve. It was a memorable day in more than one way. We had moved from the far south side of Chicago, an area called Beverly Hills, to a western suburb, Oak Park, a few months earlier. But my mother in particular wanted me to join the church I had grown up in, even though it did not follow the Baptist practice of total immersion, which she thought so important. So I was sprinkled on the head by the minister at the same time I joined the church. Perhaps as a way of celebrating the day, my father suggested we stop at Midway Airport on the way back to Oak Park and have a bite of lunch. Midway was relatively small, of course, in 1941. The lunchroom was quite informal, more like a diner, and on the wall was a radio playing. And it was here, in the early afternoon of December 7, that we heard the news that the Japanese had just bombed Pearl Harbor. The world of all Americans changed drastically from that day forward.

I was also just a year and a little more from entering high school. As I have just said, we had moved to Oak Park just a few months before this, and my teenage experience centered on new associations in Oak Park. Before this, I had absorbed mainly my parents' differing views of Christianity. To my mother, it was all about being saved from hell, about preparing for the next world. Evangelical to the core, she was also a fundamentalist, believing that every word in the Bible could be explained as true. My father was deeply religious, but more concerned with the ethical commands of Christianity than in debating the merits of personal salvation. In fact, at his funeral many years later, the minister commented that he had often thought my father should be in the pulpit instead of him. Now I became aware that there was an even wider variety of views. At a high-school Easter sunrise service, for instance, the local Congregational minister told us that Jesus had obviously not risen from the dead, but that we were celebrating something more profound than a physical reappearance.

Then one evening, later in my high school experience, I was visiting a teacher who was our adviser on the literary magazine of which I was an editor. The war was still going on, and I made some comment about the evil in the world. She said, "Do you believe that God is omnipotent?" Yes, I replied, of course, since that was what we read in the Bible. "Then," she said "how could there be any evil?" I don't remember the rest of the conversation, but when I repeated this part of it at home, my mother was appropriately shocked. This English teacher happened to be a Christian Scientist, and this short conversation was probably my first taste of the logic in the metaphysical system of Christian Science. She had gone on to say, gently, that what we know or think about God makes a big difference. You bet!

I also remember one conversation with another teacher, the drama teacher for whom I did all kinds of stage work and acted as pianist during operetta rehearsals. We were on the way to something in Chicago, and I must have asked him if he regarded himself as a Christian. "Yes," he replied, "but I certainly don't believe that Jesus was my personal savior."

So, by the time I set off for college, I was obviously aware of the different views people took toward religion, and it was a subject on my mind perhaps more than was usual for an eighteen-year-old.

* * * *

One of the most important defenses made of the importance of religion came from the philosopher and founder of American psychology, William James. James gave a series of lectures at Edinburgh University in 1901 and 1902 that were the basis of his book *The Varieties of Religious Experience*. In a letter to a friend before he gave the lectures, he noted his belief that the "real backbone" of religion was not its philosophy, but the religious experience itself. He went on to say that "I myself invincibly do believe, that, although all the special manifestations of religion may have been absurd (I mean its creeds and theories), yet the life of it as a whole is mankind's most important function." This is quoted in a lecture delivered in Japan by the religious scholar Richard Niebuhr, who went on to note that James found the religious experience important because it "exemplif[ied] an expansion of the scope of perception, a breaching of the dikes of ordinary awareness so that a much wider field of consciousness flows in." I have more to say about James later.

Something similar to this view of James's were the conclusions of C.G. Jung, one of the most influential thinkers to probe into the depths of consciousness in the last century. Jung wrote that "religion is a relation of the highest and most powerful value…that psychological fact which wields the greatest power in your system functions as a god." John Dourley put it this way: Jung located "the reality of God as that immanent power within life which offers to life its fulfillment. And he argues that when one is unaware of this power he deprives himself of this "life-giving source."

Now exactly what this power is and how it operates in our lives is in one sense the totality of what I am trying to write about. In another sense, though, one can only give intimations of this power in writing. It has to be felt, it has to be lived, and that you can do only for yourselves. But it was of prime importance to two monumental thinkers of the last century (James and Jung). I use them as examples here because neither approached this subject from a traditional theological point of view. They were not coming to the defense of what was traditional, orthodox Christianity at that time. In fact, James had little use for organized religion with its creeds, and Jung, while he praised many of the aspects of Christianity, in effect re-invented the religion in writing about it.

Richard Niebuhr, whom I have just mentioned, wrote this about Jung and Paul Tillich, the leading theologian of the mid-twentieth century: "Jung and Tillich would seem to imply in their own ways that within the depths of life with which the psychologist deals there are operative those healing and restorative powers the experience of which human beings have commonly called God."

Where did the idea of God originate? One can explain it partly from the awe that ancient peoples felt when they looked out at their universe. How did all this come to be? If they didn't ask the key question of how they came to be here, they were certainly struck by the uncertainty of life, their dependence on rain and sun for their crops and livelihood. And when they looked up at the sky, they must have felt the same wonder that comes to us all on a star-filled night. They were also struck by fear of the unknown. For centuries many peoples invested in the unknown forces that could affect their lives for good or evil—there was a rain god, a war god, a god of the harvest, a god of fertility, and so on. Because human life was at best precarious over long periods of time, it made sense to try to be in favor with, or at least to not anger, the gods who might influence one's own existence.

This particular sense of deity evolved in differing ways in different cultures. In the one we belong to, it was the Jews who first conceived of there being a single God who had created the universe and who must be obeyed. Even in many parts of the Old Testament, it is apparent that the Jews looked on God as *their* God, while acknowledging the existence of other gods whom other tribes or cultures worshipped. Gradually there emerged the concept that one omnipotent God had created and ruled the universe and therefore the gods of the other tribes must be false gods, false concepts of deity.

Throughout the Jewish and Christian scriptures, God is a being who intrudes in history. God is an active participant in the affairs of men. In a literal interpretation of some New Testament writings, he even "sends" his son Jesus to redeem man. At the same time, the Bible portrays him as being an omnipotent creator, as being wholly apart from the human situation that he created. Many biblical concepts of God cannot be literally reconciled with each other—and here is a situation that may be hard to accept—nor do they need to be. What they all point to is the belief that man is in some way connected to something bigger than himself, that his life has some meaning beyond mere physical existence, that as individuals we are all related in some way that makes our behavior toward each other, our concern for each other, a matter of vital importance. Could we get to this point without a belief in God? Yes, in today's world many have. But in a historical sense, our culture as a whole arrived at this point by believing in the God of the Bible, as the biblical concept developed from a limited God, to one omnipotent God; from a god who could be angered and was very personal, to a God who was loving and just and demanded from his creation that it also be loving and just.

The scientific revolution that began in the Renaissance years of the fifteenth and sixteenth centuries and then blossomed, particularly in Protestant northern Europe, in the seventeenth and eighteenth centuries abolished the traditional concept of God for many people. As natural scientists discovered the secrets of the physical universe, particularly its age, they lost any remaining belief they might have had in a personal God who had created it. Among scientists, those who still believed in God replaced the image of the white-bearded figure in the sky with that of a giant clockmaker. This universe is his clock; he made it and then let the laws of physics run it.

While this concept may have satisfied some of the philosophers who thought they saw all they needed of God in a universe that worked according to immutable natural laws, it did not even approach the need people felt for the traditional God to whom they had felt a personal relationship. And this lack of faith in the traditional teaching of the Church led to a loss of faith in general among large numbers of both ordinary and highly sophisticated individuals. Had they known that religious thinkers had been finding new ways to describe God in meaningful terms all through the Middle Ages, the decline of religious faith would very likely not have occurred. But I will tell you more about this in one of the following chapters.

* * * *

At this point it may be the right time to tell you how I became interested in Christian Science. It was not a sudden "conversion" at all; it was not an epiphany. My interest in it grew from a variety of sources: my two cousins who were Christian Scientists and whose general enthusiasm and zest for life had always intrigued me; my closest friend in high school (he went on to Yale and I saw him frequently during those New England years), who happened to be a Christian Scientist and whose mother was just entering the public practice of Christian Science; my freshman philosophy course at Harvard, in which we discussed the contradictions between a belief in an omnipotent God and a sinful humanity; the closeness to Boston and my visiting The Mother Church early in the autumn of my first year at Harvard.

But it was not until the next summer, when I took down my father's copy of *Science and Health* from his bookcase and began to read it, that my curiosity grew to the point where I realized that the basic concepts Mrs. Eddy was explaining, page after page, were concepts that made sense to me. There was the emphasis on knowing rather than believing. There was her definition of God, which I will discuss later on. Probably the most important concept to me at that time was her distinction between Jesus and the Christ: Very roughly put, Jesus was the human person and the Christ the divine ideal he represented to a fuller extent than any man had ever done—and as Christians believe, to the fullest extent any man ever will do.

To try to position it very roughly, Christian Science was not the liberal Protestant theology, with its emphasis on the ethical demands of Christ Jesus. Nor was it the old-fashioned evangelical Christianity, which depended on man's acceptance of the belief that he was guilty of something and had to be "saved." In a broader sense, it was both: It was demanding of one's behavior, of both one's personal and social ethics, and it was evangelical in the sense that it demanded a complete change of consciousness about what man really is.

To pursue my interest in Christian Science, I enrolled in the Sunday School at The Mother Church after Christmas vacation in January 1949. I was nineteen years old, and Christian Science Sunday Schools are available for anyone until the age of twenty. I hoped, when I enrolled, that I would be put in the class with Erwin Canham, who at that time, as editor of *The Christian Science Monitor,* was Mr. Christian Science in Boston and already a nationally known figure. I was initially disappointed. The superintendent assigned me to the class of a Boston dowager, Mrs. Gertrude Eiseman. It seemed to me that she wore the same dull navy-blue dress every Sunday, and I imagined her to be a dutiful middle-class widow doing her bit to teach us teenagers. She took a keen interest in each of the kids in her class. Learning that I was new to Science, she wrote me short letters each week, showing me how I might approach the main points in the weekly Bible Lessons we were studying. Then she occasionally invited several of us to her apartment for lunch. Two of us,

Tom Griesa, who has been a distinguished federal judge in New York for over thirty years, and I, played the piano, and we would occasionally play for her. Being a college student, away from home, these occasional visits—and meals—with her solidified a friendship that lasted until she passed on at almost the age of one hundred in 1986.

What I found out over time was that she was a very wealthy woman who had decided, after her husband had passed on, to devote the rest of her life to the study of Christian Science. She was in the public practice and kept an apartment in one of Boston's oldest hotels. She frequently had her meals brought to her room. One time, years later, my wife and I were eating with her at the Ritz Carlton in Boston. We sat talking after dinner, and then she prepared to get up and leave. I noticed that the waiter had not brought the check and asked if she needed to sign something. "Oh," she said, "they never give me a check." Of course, I had been wrong about that dull blue dress—she could have worn a new one every week! She also happened to come from a Jewish background. This fascinated me, as I realized for perhaps the first time that Christian Science can come to anyone who is ready for it and willing to take its message seriously.

Christian Science comes to people in myriad ways. Most people think of Christian Science in terms of its emphasis on spiritual healing. This quite clearly was not what interested me as a young man. It was its explanations of the nature of God and of Jesus' mission that seemed to answer the questions I had at the moment. Recently, in a conversation with an Episcopal priest, I was discussing my early interest in Christian Science. He said, "Of course, if you will forgive me, Christian Science is a great heresy. I say this because, like all heresies, it is a heresy because it overemphasizes one point."

I recognized that he was talking about spiritual healing, which is also practiced to some extent in his own church. "All right, I might agree with you to some extent," I said, "But for me, the point that Christian Science emphasizes is that spiritual reality is the only, or ultimate, reality. It made real for me St. John's vision of the new heaven and new earth in the final chapter of Revelation. It threw light on what Jesus said when he told his disciples that the kingdom of God was here—within. And in glimpsing this reality, of mentally living within it, spiritual healing becomes a natural occurrence."

Chapter Two

RALPH WALDO EMERSON

In the same years in which I was becoming acquainted with Christian Science, I had an "enabler" of sorts: the "sage of Concord," Ralph Waldo Emerson. Emerson is remembered most today for his connection with the Transcendentalists, although his long life as minister, philosopher, writer, and lecturer gives him a unique position in the history of that era. He was a Transcendentalist in the sense that all those connected with that movement thought they saw something further than the universe that the five senses presented to them, and that this "something" could be directly intuited by the human mind. But Emerson was first and foremost an individualist and cannot be directly associated with any movement. He is remembered by most people today as a writer and lecturer, although one Harvard professor, Stanley Cavell, considers him America's greatest philosopher. I tend to think of him that way myself, although his importance as a philosopher lies more in an attitude of mind than in anything formulaic.

When his writings are presented today, they will always include his Phi Beta Kappa address at Harvard in the summer of 1837. The address is regarded as his declaration of American intellectual independence. This address, now called "The American Scholar," delivered to the young men who would be the next generation's scholars, puts book learning on a high plain, but not on a pedestal. "Meek young men," he said, "grow up in libraries, believing it their duty to accept the views which Cicero, which Locke, which Bacon have given; forgetful that Cicero, Locke, and Bacon were only young men in libraries when they wrote these books." Claiming that no artist can "exclude the conventional, the local, the perishable from his book," he concluded that "each age...must write its own books; or rather, each generation for the next succeeding."

The address was also a plea to follow what one has learned from books with action: with the full development of one's character. "So much only of life as I know by experience; so much of the wilderness have I vanquished and planted, or so far have I extended my being: my dominion. I do not see how any man can afford, for the sake of his nerves and his nap, to spare any action in which he can partake. It is pearls and rubies to his discourse." And the single most important pearl that a man of character could manifest was self-trust. Urging these young men not to blindly emulate the ways of a past generation or of the older European culture, he ended with this positive note: "We will walk on our own feet; we will work with our own hands, we will speak our own minds."

This same emphasis on independence of thought is reinforced by one of his most famous essays, "Self-Reliance." Its opening lines instruct us to believe what comes to our own consciousness: "To believe your own thought to believe that what is true for you in your private heart is true for all men,—that is genius...Familiar as the voice of the mind is to each, the highest merit we ascribe to Moses, Plato and Milton is that they set at naught books and traditions, and spoke not what men, but what *they* thought."

Whether one's private intuitions are always close to the truth does not bother Emerson so much as men's reluctance to at least test their ability to stand on their own feet. He says that "imitation is suicide." He also says "...though the wide universe is full of good, no kernel of nourishing corn can come to him but through his toil bestowed on that plot of ground which is given to him to till." It is also in this essay that Emerson's famous sentence about consistency appears: "A foolish consistency is the hobgoblin of little minds...." His point is that a man must say and do what he believes today. "The voyage of the best [sailing] ship is a zigzag of a hundred tacks. See the line from a sufficient distance, and it straightens itself out to the average tendency. Your genuine action will explain itself and will explain your other genuine actions. Your conformity explains nothing."

Self-reliance, when applied to the practice of one's religion, would thus demand that one have thoughts of God that come fresh today: "If therefore a man claims to know and speak of God and carries you backward to the phraseology of some old mouldered nation in another country, in another world, believe him not. Is the acorn better than the oak which is its fulness and completion?"

But, said Emerson, "see what strong intellects dare not yet hear God himself unless he speak the phraseology of I know not what David, or Jeremiah, or Paul. We shall not always set so great a price on a few texts, on a few lives. We are like children who repeat by rote the sentences of grandames and tutors...." You can see how sentiments such as these resonated with my teenage mind. I was in the process of leaving behind some of most the trenchant religious beliefs that had been instilled in me as a child—and these are the hardest of all to give up—and yet I felt I was acting from the best within me, not from the touted insouciance with which teenagers often want to throw off the ties of home in a show of their independence. It also helped, when one of my close college friends told me one night that he and several others were concerned about my infatuation with Christian Science, to feel that, even though the main concepts of Christian Science were not original with me, it was not so unusual that I as a thinking individual might, at the moment at least, be alone in the path I was beginning to travel.

As much as I admired the attitude Emerson projected, even if it did nothing more than tell us that each one of us has the responsibility to develop our own powers and ultimately our own philosophy of living, it wasn't until my senior year in college, when I was writing my history honors thesis on an ex-Unitarian minister, Octavius Brooks Frothingham, that I realized how early in his adult life Emerson had acted on this advice.

Frothingham wrote what at the time was considered a seminal work on the history of the Transcendentalist movement, and in it he included the sermon that Waldo Emerson, at the age of twenty-nine, had delivered to his church in Boston. The year was 1832, before any of the essays were written, and it was Emerson's own example of being true to his deepest beliefs. At that time the Unitarians, although not believers in the Trinity of orthodox Christianity, still regularly practiced communion, the commemoration of Jesus' Last Supper with his disciples. From his reading of the New Testament, and undoubtedly from inner convictions that came to him as intuition, Emerson concluded that Jesus had never intended to institute this rite as a continuing memorial. Emerson felt that he could no longer administer the communion, so he resigned his pulpit at the end of this historic sermon. Robert Richardson, in his 1995 biography, *Emerson: The Mind on Fire*, notes that Emerson's resignation from the ministry was a bit more involved than this. Emerson had come to believe that the whole orthodox Christian tradition, going back to the Apostle Paul, that Jesus' sacrificial death had paid the price for humanity's fall under Adam was "absolutely incredible." Since the practice of communion was so tied to this orthodox belief, he could no longer in good conscience go along with it.

In the year 1832 the entire nineteenth-century process of biblical exegesis, in which German scholarship would take the lead, lay mostly in the future. Yet Emerson, from his own careful study of the New Testament, came to conclusions that would stand the test of further scholarship. The issue of communion may not interest you, or very many who may read this later on, but it is worth at least a brief comment here. Emerson noted that in the four Gospel accounts of Jesus' last days, there was only one suggestion that the practice should be continued. Matthew and Mark say nothing about its being suggested by Jesus—only Luke. As for John, this author, writing the farthest from Jesus in time (close to the year 100 CE), does not even mention a Last Supper. Instead, he has Jesus washing the feet of his disciples and telling them they should do this to each other. Emerson writes, almost impishly, that there exists as much authority for washing each other's feet as for communion: "Compare with it the account of this transaction in St. John, and tell me if this be not much more explicitly authorized than the Supper. It only differs in this, that we have found the Supper used in New England and the washing of the feet not." As for Luke's statement that the Last Supper be commemorated, Emerson thinks this might have been said and could have a simple explanation: "He thinks of his own impending death, and wishes the mind of his disciples to be prepared for it. 'When hereafter,' he says to them, 'you shall keep the Passover, it will have an altered aspect to your eyes. It is now a historical covenant of God with the Jewish nation. Hereafter, it will remind you of a new covenant sealed with my blood. In years to come, as long as your people shall come up to Jerusalem to keep this feast, the connection which has subsisted between us will give a new meaning in your eyes to the national festival, as the anniversary of my death.'"

What disturbed Emerson most about the ritual was that the mere repetition of an event blurred its meaning to the modern mind: "To eat bread is one thing; to love the precepts of Christ and resolve to obey them is quite another." Moreover, he found "a painful confusion of thought between the worship due to God and the commemoration due to Christ." He says, "I am so much a Unitarian as this: that I believe the human mind cannot admit but one God, and that every effort to pay religious homage to more than one being, goes to take away all right ideas. In the moment when you make the least petition to God, though it be but a silent wish that he may approve you, or add one moment to your life—do you not, in the very act, necessarily exclude all other beings from your thought? In that act, the soul stands alone with God, and Jesus is no more present in the mind than your brother or your child."

Six years after leaving the ministry, and a year after his Phi Beta Kappa address at Harvard, Emerson was asked back to give a talk to the graduating class of Harvard's Divinity School (1838). Here he used the opportunity to talk about the responsibility of the clergy to breathe new life into their own ministries. This was the era of the Second Great Awakening, of emotional preaching in the small towns of America that gave rise to parts of New York State being called the "burned over" area—so much preaching and converting had gone on. But Emerson was talking to a group of more conservative, rationalistic young clergy.

"The stationariness of religion," he said, "the assumption that the age of inspiration is past; that the Bible is closed; the fear of degrading the character of Jesus by representing him as a man—indicate with sufficient clearness the falsehood of our theology. It is the office of a true teacher to show us that God is, not was; that He speaketh, not spake. The true Christianity—a faith like Christ's in the infinitude of man—is lost."

Christianity as Emerson saw it had made the mistake of confusing the message with the messenger who had brought it. It worshipped Jesus instead of trying to follow his example. He said, "Jesus Christ belonged to the true race of prophets.

He saw with open eye the mystery of the soul. Drawn by its severe harmony, ravished with its beauty, he lived in it, and had his being there. Alone in all history he estimated the greatness of man. One man was true to what is in you and me. He saw that God incarnated himself in man, and evermore goes forth anew to take possession of his World."

Yet, with its "noxious exaggeration about the person of Jesus, this eastern monarchy of a Christianity, which indolence and fear have built, the friend of man is made the injurer of man." Emerson urged the young ministers to go it alone, "to refuse the good models, even those which are sacred in the imagination of men, and dare to love God without mediator or veil."

At the end of his talk, he spoke words that still contain a special significance for me, although I may be reading too much into them. He said of the Bible, "The Hebrew and Greek Scriptures contain immortal sentences that have been bread of life to millions. But they have no epical integrity; are fragmentary; are not shown in their order to the intellect. I look for the new Teacher that shall follow so far those shining laws that he shall see them come full circle...." As a young Christian Scientist, it seemed to me that the Teacher had come, and that the Christian Science textbook did set forth those laws.

After this rousing speech, Emerson was not invited back to talk at the Divinity School for almost thirty years. Whether or not his talk was the only reason, one cannot know. The story may be mostly apocryphal, but undoubtedly what he said fell harshly on the ears of some of his listeners.

Exactly what the word "God" meant to Emerson is not always clear. He certainly believed in a universe not apparent to the material senses. He did not develop a complete philosophy or theology, whichever one might call it, beyond his strong belief in the capacity of each individual to take part in divinity, to hear God speaking to him in language that meant something to his experience and at the same time was a universal message. That is, we all might hear it differently, depending on our background and our individual needs, but there was still a "center" from which our individual intuitions sprang.

The closest he comes to describing his theology is in his essay "The Over-Soul." Here the otherworldliness of his vision is fairly clear: "What we commonly call man, the eating, drinking, planting, counting man, does not, as we know him, represent himself, but misrepresents himself. Him we do not respect; but the soul, whose organ he is, would he let it appear through his actions, would make our knees bend....Of this pure nature every man is at some time sensible...."

He says that we call these "announcements of the soul" *revelation*, "for this communication is an influx of the Divine mind into our mind." He thinks of man at his best as united with God: "Ineffable is the union of men and God in every act of the soul. The simplest person who in his integrity worships God, becomes God; yet for ever and ever the influx of his better and universal self is new and unsearchable...When we have broken our God of tradition and cease from our God of rhetoric, then may God fire the heart with his presence."

While God thus seems to be an objective reality to Emerson, the experience of God can only be subjective. Thus one is eventually forced into a radical reliance on his own intuitions: "...if he would know what the great God speaketh, he must 'go into his closet and shut the door,' as Jesus said...He must greatly listen to himself, withdrawing himself from all the accents of other men's devotion...He that finds God a sweet enveloping thought to him never counts his company. When I sit in that presence, who shall dare to come in?"

Emerson leaves one, at least at this stage of his own life, which was only half over, with the emphasis on each individual working things out for himself, with the affirmation of an objective God, or Mind, as he puts it in "The Over-Soul," from which to obtain guidance and an appreciation for the message of Jesus, but no confusion as to the person of Jesus. This, at least, is what my reading of Emerson meant to me years ago and still means to me today.

He did not go all the way, in terms of what I was learning in Christian Science, in the way that Science describes spiritual reality as the only reality. But a re-reading of him today serves to remind me that descriptions of spiritual things in human language are never entirely adequate and that it is what we get from any verbal description that becomes actionable in our own lives that matters. And that brings me back to Emerson's belief that following any single human model is not as good as listening to our own mature intuition.

Chapter Three

THOUGHTS ABOUT GOD AND JESUS IN THE MIDDLE AGES

I have been writing about Emerson's own description, to the extent that it really was a description, of his concept of God. Now I want to jump back six or seven centuries before the time of Emerson to some reading that I have done only in the past few years. I will try to show you the connection— why I am putting it here.

Protestants in general, to the extent that they have any historical perspective at all, tend to think of Protestantism as something that arose to clear the air both of abuses within the Church and some doctrinal errors, after a quiescent period following, let us say, St. Augustine in the fifth century. For a thousand years, nothing of note happened in Christian religious thinking, according to this simplified outlook, until Martin Luther nailed his ninety-five theses on the wall of the church in Wittenberg in 1517 and Henry VIII defied the Roman church in 1534 because it denied him a divorce. In actual fact, those thousand years were as full of religious history as political, but the textbooks we all study in school talk mainly about politics and culture. Few of us were probably ever aware, for instance, of the intermittent but never-ending persecution of the Jews by the Christian Church throughout this period of history. I first learned of this in some detail only when I read James Carroll's book, *The Sword of Constantine*, published in 2001.

What might be of particular interest to you in what I am trying to talk about right now, though, are the various ways in which the theologians and philosophers of all three major monotheistic faiths tried to develop their concepts of God in the period from about 1100 to 1300. First of all, this was a period of intense communication about the religious "elites" of that day. Muslim scholars had translated the works of Plato and Aristotle from Greek into Arabic, and their acquaintance with Greek philosophy impelled them to try to reconcile the ideas of God in Islam with the Greek philosophic ideas of deity. The Muslims controlled Spain, and for a long period the Jewish community in Spain lived in close harmony with the Muslims. Then the knowledge of Plato and Aristotle spread from Spain into France, where their philosophies were translated into Latin. Moreover, the theologians who discussed these ideas had a mutual knowledge of the positions taken by others, so there was a genuine respect for each religion. (Maimonides, the best known Jewish philosopher of the period, eventually left Spain and served as the physician for the sultan, who was Muslim, in Cairo.)

Some of this intercommunication would have occurred without the Crusades, which lasted roughly from 1090 into the 1200s. But the Crusades acted as another "enabler" of the spread of religious ideas. In his book *A History of Christian Thought*, Paul Tillich says the Crusades were not important politically or militarily, but "because they brought about the encounter of Christianity with two highly developed cultures, the original Jewish and the Islamic cultures. One could perhaps even say that a third culture was encountered at that time, namely, the classical culture of ancient Greece, which was mediated into the medieval world by the Arabian theologians. The fact of an encounter with another, if it is serious enough, always involves a kind of self-reflection." Thus, "Christianity began to reflect on itself in a much more radical way."

There are some important names in the period that deserve to be memorized and remembered as much as those of any of the kings or popes. Among the Muslims, two philosophers stand out: Avicenna (Ibn Sina—980-1037) and

Averroes (Ibn Rush—1126-1198). Among the Christians, there is Anselm of Canterbury (1033-1109) and Peter Abelard, a Frenchman (1079-1142). The Muslim and Jewish philosophers are of interest because of the ways in which they thought God could be conceived of, or known. The Christians were among the first to begin to write about Christian doctrine in ways that presaged the coming of the Reformation three or more centuries later.

The confrontation with Greek philosophy challenged these medieval thinkers to reconcile their concept of God with the Greek notions of deity. The most important point here is that they had to identify the means by which man can come to know God: through human reason, the way of the philosophers; or through revelation, which may come to only a few, such as the Hebrew prophets, Jesus, or Mohammed, or through a personal revelation that can come to anyone prepared to receive it. This latter way is the way of the mystics, and every major religion has within it groups of people who are more able practitioners of the mystical approach than the average man or woman seems to be.

None of these people questioned whether God exists—whether there is a God. But they wanted to know more about him, or it, and the methods they pursued and the answers they got were diverse. The Muslim thinkers who tried to reconcile reason with the Koran were called *Faylasufs*. Educated for their day, part of the scientific advances taking place in the Muslim world of 1000 CE, they felt that religion should not be relegated to a separate sphere. They believed that the entire universe is rational—therefore the human mind should be able to arrive at the same knowledge of God that had come through revelation. And it was Avicenna whom we remember as the most important exponent of this point of view. Karen Armstrong summarizes his thinking this way: "Something must have started the chain of cause and effect. The absence of such a supreme being would mean that our minds were not in sympathy with reality as a whole. That, in turn, would mean that the universe was not coherent and rational. This utterly simple being upon which the whole of multiple, contingent reality depended was what the religions called 'God.' Because it is the highest thing of all, it must be absolutely perfect and worthy of honor and worship."

Avicenna turned more toward mysticism in his later years. Yet he stands as a prime example of the attempt to reconcile the type of reasoning the Greek philosophers had used with the intuitions of the "religions of the book" that come through revelation.

An opponent of this approach to God was al-Ghazzali (1058-1111). He spent a good part of his life learning the approach of the Faylasufs and then rejecting them. He then spent ten years living as a Sufi (mystic) and became convinced that their way led to an intuitive knowledge. As Armstrong puts it, al-Ghazzali concluded that the mystical experience of the Sufis "was the only way of verifying a reality that lay beyond the reach of the human intellect and cerebral process."

The approach of the Faylasufs found support mostly from Averroes, who lived a couple of generations after the time of al-Ghazzali. His commentaries on Aristotle were translated into Hebrew and Latin, and it was through Averroes that this attempt to reconcile Greek thought, particularly that of Aristotle, with Christianity, spread to northern Europe. Its influence made itself felt most, during the thirteenth century, in the work of Albert the Great (1200-1280) and Thomas Aquinas (1225-1274).

In these and other thinkers of the eleventh and twelfth centuries we see the same questions being raised that Mary Baker Eddy, without benefit of formal theological training or knowledge, wrestled with in articulating the vision of reality that came to her as Christian Science. Can unaided human reason reach the truth? What or who exactly is God? Does an intellectual definition of God have any practical significance without the direct individual experience of God? And, although I have not discussed it here, these same people wrestled with the dilemma of how an infinite God could have created a material universe.

At the same time that there was ferment in the religious thought of Muslims and Jews in southern Europe, there was a stirring going on among some individuals in the Christian North. This would become stronger with the founding of the first universities in leading centers of the continent. But for the moment, consider two persons of this period who had thoughts that resonate and can challenge thinkers today—Anselm and Abelard.

Anselm became the archbishop of Canterbury in 1093. However, he fell out of favor with the English king over several issues and spent much of his time in exile in Rome. He is interesting here because, like some of the Muslim thinkers I have mentioned, he also thought considerably about the relationship of faith and reason. He said he wrote in the spirit of *fides quaerens intellectum,* or "faith seeking understanding." Like the Muslims, he did not think he had to prove the existence of God, which he took for granted, but he wanted that faith to be one that did not contradict his human reason. In developing his concept of God, he used the following argument: Since we see varying degrees of goodness in the world, there must be some standard of goodness. Similarly, we see varying degrees of perfection, suggesting that there must be some absolute perfection. Finally, we see that effect follows cause; therefore there must be some ultimate cause. Therefore, for a Christian, the word God means "the highest good, the original cause and the infinite perfection." These proofs for God could be argued against, of course, and they were, even at the time. But the terms of the discussion show that for these thinkers, God was a more universal, spiritual concept than could be conveyed by the popular conceptions of a God made in the image of human beings.

As for Anselm's "faith seeking understanding," what he appears to believe becomes clearer from the translation of the Latin words *Credo ut intellegum*—I believe *in order* to understand. The word *Credo* at the time meant not a passive belief in some doctrine, but an intellectual grappling with it, or grasping it, since only in the grasping or taking hold of it was it possible *to* understand. Paul Tillich said something similar, in this case talking about the faith of St. Bernard: "Faith is daring and free, an anticipation of something which can become real personally *only through full experience*. Certainty is not given in the act of faith; it is a daring anticipation of a state to which one may attain. Faith is created by the divine Spirit, and the experience which follows confirms it."

Let us look at another continental thinker of the period— Abelard (1079-1142). He is described by one religious scholar as being "usually rather conventional" in his theological views, but David Chidester calls him "the most controversial scholar of twelfth century Europe." (He is also remembered in literature because of his early love affair with Eloise and its disastrous consequences.) What may have caused Abelard the most trouble was his work on a treatise called *Sic et Non (Yes and No)*, a work in which he contrasted some of the statements of faith attributed to the early Church fathers. This seemed to show that there had been disagreement early on over some matters of faith. Abelard fell into disfavor with St. Bernard of Clairvaux, who was perhaps the most prominent French churchman of the century. He was called before a Church council, at which he was vehemently attacked by Bernard. Abelard, already not well, is reported to have collapsed at the council. He died a year later.

Besides Abelard's work in analyzing the early Church fathers, the kind of work that was the beginning of stirrings within the Church that would increasingly cause it to examine itself and its teachings, he interests me because of the novel approach (for his time) to the purpose of Jesus' mission. Abelard rejected the Augustinian doctrine of original sin descending from Adam's disobedience. He maintained that Jesus came neither to pay a ransom for the rest of mankind nor to save humans from the devil. He held, instead, that Jesus' life was "the embodiment of perfect Love" and that by setting this example for mankind he had become its savior. This is close to the theology of what eventually evolved as liberal Protestant Christianity and shows that such intellectual ferment was alive as early as the twelfth century.

Chapter Four

A CONCEPT OF GOD FOR TODAY

A. N. Wilson is a British literary critic, editor, and author. Besides writing several novels, he has written biographies of Jesus, Paul, and Tolstoy. His 1999 book, *God's Funeral,* is an account of what he calls the loss of faith in Britain during the nineteenth century. This was the period during which the scientific revolution took hold of the human intellect, with the result that many of the prescientific accounts of creation and of God's intervention in human affairs no longer seemed tenable to thinking persons. This forced them to choose one path or the other—that of the conventional Christianity of their day, or the new view of the rationalists and scientists. Wilson writes in fascinating detail about the angst felt by many of Britain's intellectuals in both the fields of theology and literature.

The crisis was both individual and societal. On the personal level, Wilson writes, "Is our personal religion that which links us to the ultimate reality, or is it the final human fantasy, the most pathetic demonstration, in a spiritually empty, spatially limitless universe, of human aloneness? Is prayer the last existential pathos?" These were questions that could perhaps never have a final, authoritative answer, but which each individual, including us today, has to ask and answer for himself or herself.

On a societal level, the question involved the basics of morality. "Is there a world of value outside ourselves, or do we, collectively and individually, invent what we call 'The Good?' Is there an objective transcendent truth in these areas, as we believe there is in physical science, or is there only an inner mystical 'truth,' where inverted commas are always needed if we are not to proclaim lies?"

The personal anguish that so many thinkers felt as they dealt with these questions can be explained in large part by the traditional views they had held of God. While any thinking person knew that God was not the white-bearded man in the sky, it was difficult to conceive of the God who had spoken to Moses on Mount Sinai in any terms other than personal ones. If fairly well-educated citizens in the nineteenth century had been aware of even some of the thinking on the part of religious and philosophic scholars that had gone on throughout the Middle Ages, for instance, they very well might have had less trouble adjusting to the relationship of science and religious authority in their lives. They would not have been stuck with a "model" of God in their own thought that they could no longer believe.

The theologians of the eleventh and twelfth centuries who had tried to reconcile the God of Aristotle with the personal God of Judaism and Christianity had, to a large degree, come to a dead end, as the last chapter showed. Western Christianity had more and more taken the path of requiring adherence to a set doctrine, and disagreement over this doctrine and the authority of those who proclaimed it had led to the Protestant Reformation and to the later subdivisions within Protestantism. Yet, outside of Western Christianity, the path had led in another direction. For want of a better overall description, the mystics had become increasingly important in Islam, Judaism, and the Eastern Christian church. No religious person of that era doubted the existence of God. But the debates over his essence, sparked by the collision with Greek thought, had led many to decide that God could be recognized only within the heart of each individual. This did not mean that we each have our own individual God, but that we conceive of him and in some sense experience his presence in ways unique to each of us.

The approach of the mystic was unique to each faith. But in common with them all was the fact that the practice of knowing God, or of feeling his presence, was one that had to be cultivated. Karen Armstrong makes a particular point of this, that true mysticism is, in psychological terms, an altered state of consciousness and not to be toyed with, as one might do some physical exercise for thirty minutes a day. (The chapter on William James will consider his views on states of consciousness.) In Greek Orthodoxy, mysticism had been brought down to the level of the ordinary mortal through the use of icons and other rituals that were reminders of the presence of deity.

Western Christianity still had to discard the pseudoscientific myths of God's creation of this material universe, of Adam's fall, or of God's speaking personally to his people. At the same time, if those myths were seen as not scientific fact, but more as legends or metaphors, the way would have been opened up to consider the spiritual truths or lessons they might illustrate. The theologians of the Middle Ages, whom I have briefly talked about in Chapter Three, could never agree on whether God had created this world *ex nihilo*—out of nothing—or whether it had always existed. Instead of describing God as a Supreme Being who had made this physical world, the approach of some of the mystics had been to conceive of God as Being itself. If this Being was supreme, there was no place for any other being. Everything that existed must be a reflection or manifestation of this Being. This was not the only approach of the mystical tradition, but it was one that satisfied those who followed it. Furthermore, it bypassed the question of how this material universe came into being. It made it possible to feel the presence of God and to know what God's demands of us are.

Did this mean that the mystic was making up his or her own God? Certainly no serious theologian would have had the egotism to say or think a thought like that. What is necessary in order to appreciate this approach, I think, is to acknowledge that everything we think we know about God came through the human consciousness of someone. God did not come down to Mount Sinai in person to speak with Moses. But Moses had a strong sense of the presence of God and of his demands on his people. God did not speak personally with Mohammed, although Mohammed's sense of God's presence was so strong that he felt the words of the Koran were being dictated. Jesus, the bedrock of every Christian's faith, dwelled so constantly in the sense of being God's child that he felt emboldened to proclaim his message. What the mystic was saying was that each of us must find God for himself. This sounds a bit like Emerson, does it not?

* * * *

When I was nine or ten years old, I was playing with two of my cousins at their house one evening. At some point, over whatever incident I do not recall, I exclaimed, "Oh my God." The playing stopped; my cousins acted as if I had struck them with a thunderbolt. They called their mother and said, "Mom, Richard just said—." A discussion ensued, and at the conclusion of it my aunt agreed that she would not tell my mother about my transgression if I solemnly agreed never to say those words again. (I suspect she told her in secret, however.)

I had forgotten about this, of course, but somewhere in the back—or at the bottom—of consciousness it was still lurking. What brought it up out of the recesses of consciousness was a talk I heard by a Unitarian minister at Chautauqua a few summers ago. The minister, David Weissbard, from Rockford, Illinois, had written a manuscript on what he thought the Ten Commandments mean for us today. When he came to the Third Commandment, "Thou shalt not take the name of the Lord thy God in vain," it popped up. Over the years I had grown careless and had repeated those words many a time as a simple exclamation. I am no longer concerned that God is listening to my words, but I would agree that simple good taste would and should find a better way to express one's emotions. Weissbard cut to the core of this commandment. It is not the words we use, he said, that dishonor God, but our acts. What Moses was telling his people was that they should not appeal to the name of God without a serious sense of God's majesty. It is not profanity as such that dishonors God, but lip service to God. Religion, he said, does not consist of empty observance of some rules, but is a way of life.

Buckminster Fuller said that one should consider God not as a noun, but as a verb. The advantage in this may lie in the effect it has on our consciousness of God, not as a static being, but in terms of what God demands of us. If God is the chief actor, or the only actor, in a universe in which he is Being itself, what is the nature of his acts? What should be the nature of our acts, as individual reflections of and actors for this God?

The Canadian scholar, Northrop Frye, writing in his book *The Great Code*, agrees with Fuller: "In Exodus 3:14, though God also gives himself a name, he defines himself...as 'I am that I am,' which scholars say is more accurately rendered 'I will be what I will be.' That is, we might come closer to what is meant in the Bible by the word 'God' if we understood it as a verb, and not a verb of simple asserted existence but a verb implying a process accomplishing itself."

Paul Tillich, the German theologian who spent the greater part of his life in America and is generally regarded as the leading theologian of the twentieth century, spoke of God as the ground of being. This may not sound like much to your ears. It certainly does not sound like the God who spoke in a cloud to Moses in the Bible story. What this concept gets at, though, as far as I have tried to consider it, is that we no longer try to "prove" the existence of God to ourselves or anyone else. God is where we start, and if the ways we are led to think about God give stability and purpose to our lives, this alone is the proof. The prophet Isaiah (33:22) wrote, "For the Lord is our judge, the Lord is our lawgiver, the Lord is our king; he will save us." This verse incidentally combines all three functions of government, as Western democracies have developed them!

The Bible often refers to God's power and presence. Mrs. Eddy often refers to God similarly. For instance, "The three great verities of Spirit—omnipotence, omnipresence, omniscience—God possessing all power, all presence, all science, contradict forever the belief that matter can be actual." This is in line with the mystics' position that God should not be primarily considered as the supreme Being, but as Being itself. If God is Being, then all creation consists of that Being reflecting itself.

The most helpful part of the definition of God in Christian Science is probably the seven synonyms for Him that Mrs. Eddy used: Six of them, Life, Truth, Love, Spirit, Soul, and Mind, come directly from the Bible, and the seventh, Principle, is implied by the others, since God is the supreme lawgiver. These synonyms as mere words do nothing to increase one's spirituality, but they give the seeker after God a clue where to look. Their power is only in what they come to mean to one who uses them.

I wrote in a previous book, *The New Birth of Christianity*, that God, as "the divine Mind, is the cause of every manifestation of true intelligence in the universe. The activity of this divine Mind is synonymous with Life. God is not a static being. He is the fountain of all life...What is God's relationship to what he has created? Love alone can express this aspect of the nature of God. It is a love that includes the highest human sense of compassion, although divine Love, God, can perhaps be best glimpsed from our human standpoint as the wholeness, completeness, perfection, and oneness or unity of all that God beholds...." Truth and Love as synonyms both suggest that, God being omnipotent, they can have no opposites: Love conquers hatred; Truth recognizes, tolerates, no error. Spirit suggests the omnipresence of this divine Mind. Soul, as a synonym for God, establishes the sense of one's identity, an individual existence that cannot be separated from its Maker. (For we commonly use soul to indicate the core of our being. In this case, Mrs. Eddy is saying that our essential identity, or ego, exists in God.) Truth, if God is indeed omnipotent, implies that there is and can be no error. And Principle indicates not only that it applies to these other six synonyms, but also to the foundational, bedrock-like nature of God's being.

If we exist "in" God, where then is God? Is God immanent or transcendent? These questions pose difficult choices, and this is where mere logic breaks down. Not only Christian Scientists, but Christians in general, would say that God is *both* immanent and transcendent. That is, he is within us or around us and also the supreme Being that transcends or is above us. The easiest way to catch a glimpse of what this might mean is to look on God, as some of the medieval mystics did, as Being itself—similar but I don't think the same thing that Tillich meant when he called God the ground of being. This comes close to what the philosophers call monism, the belief or theory, according to my Random House dictionary, "holding that there is only one basic substance or principle as the ground of reality or that reality, consists of a single element."

As an aside to this immanence versus transcendence question, the Jewish philosopher Abraham Heschel quotes Arthur North Whitehead, who was a leading American philosopher early in the last century: "The Hebrews of the Old Testament certainly had a transcendent concept of God. The more immanent form is illustrated in Greek philosophy. The problem for Western man is that the history of Western thought consists in the attempted fusion of ideas which in their origin are predominantly Hellenic, with ideas which in their origin are predominantly Semitic."

Heschel also mentions, on this subject of trying to define God, that religions are always "in perpetual danger of giving primacy to concepts and dogmas and to forfeit the immediacy of insights, to forget that the known is but a reminder of God, that the dogma is a token of His will, the expression of the inexpressible at the minimum." When we call God ineffable, for instance, what we really mean is "that aspect of reality which by its very nature lies beyond our comprehension, and is acknowledged by the mind to be beyond the scope of the mind," says Heschel. This, I think, is what Mrs. Eddy meant when she wrote in *Science and Health with Key to the Scriptures* that "God, good, is self-existent and self-expressed, though indefinable as a whole."

If we have already identified God as Spirit, then all that reflects God must be spiritual. Where does this leave matter and the entire material cosmos? Here it becomes clear that for Mrs. Eddy this material universe was not what really matters. She was writing, one should remember, in the era that was only beginning to come to grips with what the Darwinian theory of evolution—and it was evolution without any final product in mind—meant to traditional religious beliefs in the Christian tradition. Yet Mrs. Eddy could write in her preface to *Miscellaneous Writings*:

> If worlds were formed by matter,
>   And mankind from the dust;
> Till time shall end more timely,
>   There's nothing here to trust.

> Thenceforth to evolution's
> > Geology, we say,—
> Nothing have we gained therefrom,
> > And nothing have to pray:
>
> My world has sprung from Spirit,
> > In everlasting day;
> Whereof, I've more to glory,
> > Wherefor, have much to pay.

Her concept of God included all the elements of God's majesty of which the biblical patriarchs had conceived. It also is similar to the philosopher's monism—God is All, and all that exists is God's reflection. This metaphysics, William James would say later, made sense only if it had a practical result. The philosophical world had just about come to the end of its enchantment with metaphysical systems. The difference here is that for Mrs. Eddy the concept of God as All had immediate practical results. She applied this revelation that she felt she had received to the healing of disease and of any discordant condition, physical or mental, and ultimately societal, that did not conform to the perfection of God.

I am certain that one element that attracted me to Christian Science was that it kept intact Jesus' message, but avoided the arguments over evolution that had plagued traditional Christianity during the nineteenth century—and still make the fundamentalists quake. This was the kingdom that Jesus had proclaimed—a realm of spiritual reality that was not readily apparent, but that would become apparent through mankind's bringing it about in individual human experience. This does not satisfy the inquiring intellect that tries to conceive of the truth of this at the same time it is considering the fossils in rocks that are millions of years old. This is an intellectual puzzle that in my own experience I simply had to let go of. What matters more in one's religion is that one can make an honest commitment to its basic approach and feel that it integrates and vitalizes one's own experience.

As for God being Truth, where does this leave error? sin? hatred? How does one account for all the evil in our world, for the physical disturbances such as the 2004 tsunami in South Asia, for the moral hideousness of 9/11 in America, or for all the hatred, envy, and jealousy in many a human heart? Christian Science again would take one back to the basic definition of God as ultimate Being. This Being did not create a material world. But Christian Science does not tell one to neglect this world, as an ascetic might, but to apply what it calls the facts of being, such as the omnipotence of God as Truth, to the human situation and help resolve some aspect of the human dilemma. (One factor that attracted me to Christian Science and led me to take financially unexplainable moves when I came to work for *The Christian Science Monitor* twice in my working years was the fact that the *Monitor's* very existence epitomized for me the Christian duty to go out into the world and help it.)

How does God appear to me from day to day? I feel that God gives me the thoughts I need each day. One can call this an inner voice, but not if that means it is something subjective. God's commands are laws; he is still the God on Mount Sinai thundering the Ten Commandments. He is the God who loves me as in the Twenty-third Psalm. At night, if I lie awake with problems I cannot let go of, I often find myself repeating the words of this Psalm or Mrs. Eddy's poem "Mother's Evening Prayer."

In the end, God must be experienced. We do not merely believe. It is a combination, as Anselm perceived in the eleventh century, of taking hold, through belief at first, and seeing what follows.

Chapter Five

ESCHATOLOGY—THE MEANING OF JESUS

[The largest part of this chapter is adapted from a lecture I delivered in Florida and California in 1999. The lecture represented an attempt to summarize some of the current research and the conclusions scholars were drawing from it on the life and mission of Jesus. More books and authors are mentioned in this material than in the rest of this book, since I was trying to draw from several sources and give each the credit due.]

Developing Images of Jesus in the First Century

This talk has developed from a good deal of current reading and research I have been doing. I find it all very useful in getting a clearer picture of Jesus, and I hope that you will also. But because I am close to what I have been doing, it is just possible that some of it may seem to jump around. First, I need to say a word about current research, going all the way back to Albert Schweitzer's book of a century ago, which for a time seemed to be the final word on Jesus research. Then, before proceeding with the developing views of Jesus during the first century of our era, there is a section on eschatology—what that word means and the different kinds of eschatology. That is a necessary precede. After that, we will look at four or five views or emphases placed on Jesus' life, and then end with a section on the role that healing played in early Christianity. I have prepared a fairly detailed outline, and that will help you follow my talk and later on, if you care, to remember some of the details. So first a word on the state of research on Jesus.

The Background

Schweitzer, in his book of 1906, summarized a century of research, largely German, into the life of Jesus. It was Schweitzer's conclusion that Jesus had come preaching the end of the world as we knew it, and that the failure of that event to happen, or for Jesus to return, had forced a reinterpretation of the Christian message. Schweitzer was writing in the decade before the civilized world entered almost half a century of world wars. It became common to accept the view that not a lot more was to be found out about the historical Jesus. Typical of this viewpoint was the work of Oscar Cullmann, another theologian from the French-German border area. Cullmann, who wrote his major books in the 40s and 50s, said that we must accept the New Testament on its own terms to understand what it was saying to us. "History in general," he thought, "is only the working out of the plan of salvation made known and realized in the particular history of the New Testament." Such a view would not likely lead to more detailed study of the origin or background to the New Testament Gospels. At the opposite end of this spectrum was the work of Rudolf Bultmann. Bultmann also agreed that "the historical Jesus himself remains in impenetrable shadow." But rather than accept the Gospels on Cullmann's terms, Bultmann said that for Christianity to have meaning for modern man it must be what he called "demythologized." He said that "the Christian message must be disengaged from the form in which it is presented in the New Testament." How he proceeded to do this, and in the process become probably the most discussed and influential theologian of his generation, is not today's subject. My point here is that this approach would also not lead to more research into the historical Jesus.

I do not know what all the steps were that led to this virtual renaissance of the study of Jesus, but the past generation has seen a virtual explosion of new interest in the subject, and the partial results of that work are what I am going to talk about now.

Eschatology

This big word is defined as that branch of theology dealing with last things—death, punishment, and the final judgment. You can see from its definition that it follows a line of thought that was ingrained into traditional Christianity for centuries. It comes into focus in this talk for two reasons: This being a millennium year, both that word and "apocalyptic" are in the air, and there is a difference between the two. The other reason is that there are different kinds of eschatology, and we are going to see an example of them in the early versions of the Jesus story.

Eschatology deals with final ends, yes; but too often we may have confused its use with the apocalypse, which is only one kind of final end that can be conceived. In his discussion of this in his book *The Birth of Christianity*, John Dominic Crossan lays out three kinds of eschatology: the apocalyptic, the ethical, and the ascetic. In the preaching of John the Baptist we have the best example of the first kind. John preached the ending of the world as we know it, a final judgment on mankind for its sins. Whether this was to be a fiery end to earth or, in less Dantean terms, a judgment of God on mankind after which the godly would rule here, the main feature of it is that the apocalypse and its timing would be the work of God. Much of current New Testament scholarship is concerned with whether this is the eschatology that Jesus actually adopted or whether his was an ethical eschatology.

The ethical type is characterized by two elements: The kingdom comes because of the actions of men, not of God; and, more important, it can be considered as already present, at least in its incipiency. That is, we experience the kingdom of God one by one, and as we reform our own lives or live them by a different standard than the world's culture dictates, we help to make the kingdom of God a reality for all mankind.

The third kind is what Crossan calls an ascetic eschatology: It is a denial of the fleshly world and goes back in time to the first chapter of Genesis. This is not identical to what Mrs. Eddy saw as the kingdom of heaven, but rather is more like the Gnostic philosophy that was evolving at the same time as Christianity. The Gnostics actually believed there had been a time of spiritual perfection that had been lost with the creation of a material universe, and that somehow we had to pass back into that former time. At least the current understanding of Gnosticism is that it represented not an attempt to transform present experience as much as an attempt to withdraw from this world. In any case, Crossan looks on Jesus as preaching an ethical eschatology. This of course requires that some of Jesus' more austere comments about the coming of the kingdom are regarded as being not his own words, but the views of those who still looked for an apocalyptic end to the oppression of the Jews by the Greek culture and Roman government under which they then lived.

Another way of defining these three eschatologies is to place their occurrence in time. The apocalypse, which awaits God's intervention, is something that will happen in the future, albeit perhaps very soon. The Gnostic, on the other hand, wants in effect to go back in time. Crossan writes, "The Gospel of Thomas is about returning to that inaugural moment at the dawn of creation, before sin, before serpent, before split. It is about paradise regained from the past, not about Parousia [Christ's Second Coming] awaited in the future." But the third, the kingdom of heaven that is reached through an ethical eschatology, can be present right now—it just depends on you and me.

The Sources

Where this comes into play in this talk is in the first two documents to be discussed that tell us what the early Christian community thought about Jesus. That is, the famous Q source, which no one has ever seen, and the Gospel of Thomas, which probably first appeared in written form in the second century. Q, as many of you know, is the presumed source of much of the material in Matthew and Luke, since so many portions of those Gospels are identical word for word that it is impossible to think that they were anything but a copying of some other *written* text. And since we can date Matthew and Luke to approximately 80 or 90 CE, we can conclude that Q was written down closer to the actual time of Jesus. Thomas was originally thought to be a second-century source, largely because it has Gnostic connotations. However, Helmut Koester, a German scholar at Harvard who built his early reputation on the thesis that many of the presumed second-century documents were actually first written closer to the time of Jesus than were the canonical Gospels, believes that Thomas was in circulation much earlier and that the present Gospel of Thomas is a second-century redaction in which the Gnostic leanings are additions. In the same way, Crossan believes that the Q source has apocalyptic references that were not a part of Jesus' message. This in turn leads us one step farther back into the labyrinth, to another unseen document that no one has yet uncovered called "The Common Sayings Tradition." The justification for thinking that this existed is the similarity between so many of the statements in the Q source and the Gospel of Thomas. And that is as far back as Crossan, at least, thinks we can go to find what the original record looks like.

This kind of textual sleuthing is similar to what a restorer of paintings would do in finding the original paint on a canvas.

He might very carefully remove the varnish on top and then experiment to see if a different color of pigment lay beneath what now appears to be the surface. I would like to emphasize that, in my judgment, most of this work is being done by believers—that is, they are not looking at Christianity from the outside nor are they ignorant of its theological underpinnings over the ages; rather they are committed Christians of many backgrounds sincerely trying to discover what the core of Jesus' life was all about.

So, in this case, having convinced themselves that much of the Q source consists of later additions that have an apocalyptic slant and that Thomas went off on a Gnostic bent in the second century, what remains? A good part of Q and Thomas have similar materials, and what they point to in Jesus' teaching are largely wisdom sayings, including some parables, that teach that the kingdom of heaven is imminent, but that its coming depends on us as individuals. I find this comforting and also feel that it sounds right. A short course my wife and I took on the first-century writing, when it discussed Q, emphasized the commands of Jesus, but also seemed harsh in talking about the coming judgment. What we know about Jesus' tenderness, which probably comes through more in Luke when we get to that, seems at odds with the harshest statements in Q. It seems to make sense that these belong to a later redaction of Q.

What, then, are these wisdom sayings? They represent an almost complete reversal of the way men lived two thousand years ago. The meek shall inherit the earth. Those who have must take care of those who do not have. He initiates a common shared meal, a sign of egalitarianism. He works with women. He says he has not come to ignore the law, but is more interested in carrying out its spirit than its letter.

It is not a kingdom over which Jesus has a monopoly. As Crossan writes, "...it is for anyone with courage enough to accept it. Jesus announces its presence, its abiding permanent possibility. He does not initiate its existence. He does not control its access. It is the kingdom, not of Jesus, but of God." The teaching, most emphatically, was not about *himself*.

Most of the current material on the decade in which Jesus worked, the 20s CE, emphasizes the turmoil that Galilee was in. Nazareth lay only four miles from Sepphoris, a city only twenty miles from Tiberias. These cities had been erected for the glory of the Roman Empire within twenty years of each other, and they had turned the rural economy of the area upside down. Many peasants had lost their small land holdings, and when Jesus talks about the poor, he is not talking mainly about those who are habitually at the bottom rung of the economic ladder, but about people who are newly dispossessed of what little they had. Jesus himself may have come from such a family, as those who practiced a craft such as woodworking were considered even lower socially than the smallest landholder. (When Jesus talked about leaving family for the sake of the kingdom, he was probably not advising walking away from one's obligations, but was showing a way to build a new community among like people who had already been dispossessed of the ties of family.)

One other facet of this discussion of Q: It does refer to John the Baptist, in much the same way as the references to him in the Gospels. But did John and Jesus preach the same thing? John preached the apocalypse. So when Jesus said that there was no greater prophet than John, but that the least in the kingdom of heaven was greater than John, was this possibly a rejection of John's definition of the kingdom? Was Jesus saying that his, Jesus', kingdom would not be brought about by an apocalyptic act of God, but by human beings who set about, with God's help, to build this new kind of kingdom?

Other writers on the Q material claim that when Jesus challenged the temple, as he did in the days preceding the crucifixion, it was a challenge not to Judaism, but to the temple elite who were aligned with the ruling powers. He was saying that the temple did not mediate man's relationship to God, but that the relationship was a direct one. Thus his challenge to the temple was almost destined to produce a crisis for him

Marcus Borg sums up Jesus' teaching as consisting of five parts: man's direct relationship to God; the wisdom sayings, and the social outlook, both of which turned conventional wisdom and the present Jewish ruling class upside down; healing; and the building of a new community. Although early Christians identified Jesus as the Messiah, Borg does not believe there is a very strong case for believing that Jesus identified himself as the Messiah. Of course, this would mean that all the references in the Gospels indicating otherwise were redactions from a later generation.

The Gospels and Paul

So much for Q. Of course we know about Q from what is more or less identical in Matthew and Luke, but before we get to those two Gospels, we need to look at Mark, written probably around 70 CE, after the destruction of the temple. The descriptions in the thirteenth chapter are what make some scholars think that the temple had already been destroyed, as they seem to be predicting just that event. Whether or not that is a correct deduction, Mark is known for its description of Jesus as the suffering Messiah. Persecution of the Christians had begun in the early 60s, and while the Gospel was written partly to give some outline of Jesus' life, it also appears to be an attempt to reinforce the faith of persecuted Christians, wherever they may be. Mark shows us a Jesus who knew he had to suffer. He begins his story of Jesus in the first chapter, with a brief reference to his temptation in the wilderness, by stressing that he was with the wild beasts. This is possibly an illusion to the fact that the early Christian martyrs were thrown to the wild beasts in the stadiums in Rome. All through the Gospel is the strain that the kingdom Jesus is talking about is worth struggling for, even suffering for. When two of the disciples ask if they can sit on his right hand in the kingdom, he asks them if they can drink of the cup he is going to drink of. (This is repeated in Matthew, but not in Luke.)

Mark is the work of someone who did not know Greek well. It is written poorly, in other words. It also seems to be explaining Jewish ways to a gentile audience—as for instance in identifying Isaiah as "the prophet," or when talking about Capernaum, saying that it is in Galilee, something any Jew would have known. The Gospel marks the first attempt to set down the events of Jesus' ministry in some kind of order, an order of events that is followed by Matthew and Luke. The first generation had passed away, and besides the fact of persecution, it was necessary to begin to record some of the events of Jesus' life as well as his teachings.

Now, Matthew and Luke were written from ten to twenty years later, and each of them was written for a different audience. By the time Matthew wrote, probably around 85 CE, the "Jesus movement" people were being thrown out of the synagogues. Up until this time, the followers of Jesus had, at least in many towns, continued to worship in the synagogues for at least a generation after the time of Jesus. Now we are almost sixty years removed from that period. This is not as strange as it may sound to modern ears, if one considers that Karen King, a professor of early Christianity at the Harvard Divinity School, doubts that Jesus intended starting a new religion as much as purifying his culture's Judaism. Christian theology was beginning to develop. There remained the differences between the Pauline Jews and the more orthodox Jews over whether Christians needed to be circumcised or obey the Jewish dietary rules. It was a time of decision for those Jews who had become Christian. Matthew is believed to have been written for Jews—some say for rich Jews, because of a few things Matthew omits—to prove to them that Jesus was the new Moses, that there was no going back to the old Judaism.

Matthew achieved this in many ways. First, in the birth story, he traces Jesus' lineage back to Abraham, father of the race. Then, in the story of Jesus' parents taking him to Egypt, he repeats the pattern of Moses' life. Moses was spared from being killed when the pharaoh was killing the Jewish infants; Jesus was spared when Herod did the same thing. Then Jesus came back from Egypt just as Moses had done at the start of the journey into the Promised Land. Jesus' face shone after the transfiguration—Matthew is the only Gospel that contains that story. Moses' face shown when he descended from Mount Sinai. Many of the events of Jesus' life are shown to coincide with events that were prophesied in the Hebrew Scriptures: At least eight times something that happens is explained by the phrase "that the scripture might be fulfilled."

Most important, perhaps, is the difference in the birth stories in Matthew and Luke. Mark, as I mentioned, begins only with Jesus' public ministry. In Matthew, Jesus is recognized as "king of the Jews" from the beginning. The wise men ask, "Where is he that is born king of the Jews?" The wise men, incidentally, are not Jewish, and one scholar says this is also Matthew's way of saying, "Look, others have recognized his kingship before you Jews." And what do the wise men bring? Gold, frankincense, and myrrh—the gold representing a worldly king, the frankincense a priestly king, and the myrrh a suffering Messiah (as myrrh was used in embalming). Matthew was saying in effect, "Whatever kind of king or messiah you are looking for, he is it."

How much modern scholars read into the Gospels! And we are not impudent in asking, How much is correct? At the very least, it seems clear that the Gospels are more sophisticated documents than most of us grew up thinking. Not every conclusion a modern-day scholar makes may be correct, but it is obvious when one approaches the Gospels analytically and with some knowledge of the times of Jesus that each Gospel did present a particular view of Jesus and had a particular audience in mind. Exactly *how* the Gospels fit into early Christian teaching or worship is not actually known.

So what was the view of Luke? First of all, Luke wrote to still a different audience—the people at large, and probably a gentile audience for the most part. But two kinds of stories predominate in Luke—his sense of Jesus' love and forgiveness, and his feeling that wealth was an impediment to gaining the kingdom. To start with the birth story, where we just left off in Matthew, Luke has no wise men from the East. Instead, Jesus is born humbly, in a manger; shepherds are nearby tending their flocks.

Two of the most memorable parables appear only in Luke: the Good Samaritan and the Prodigal Son. The Good Samaritan story is layered with metaphor. The Samaritans were like second cousins to the Jews, having split off some centuries earlier. There is no enemy in religion like the one who is closest to you, but does not agree with you. So Jesus was taking a great risk in having the man be rescued by a Samaritan. This amounts to saying, "Look, the kingdom is for everyone, even Samaritans." Even more important, perhaps, it is the Samaritan who performs the kindly act, who goes several extra steps, taking the man to the inn and offering to pay his expenses upon his return. It is the Samaritan, not the priest, who is the hero.

In the story of the Prodigal Son, there is the emphasis on forgiveness. Some also think that the two sons represent Judaism and the Jesus movement, with the older son, representing Judaism, resenting the attention given to the younger son. But God says his love has not departed from the older son either. I do not know how generally that metaphor is accepted, but certainly the story is clear about the need for forgiveness.

There is Jesus' concern for response to the human need, wherever it is—thus the parable about the importunate neighbor knocking at midnight for three loaves of bread.

Finally, this is the Gospel in which Jesus forgives one of the other men with whom he is dying and tells him he will be with him in heaven that day. Is this not saying that it is never too late to enter the kingdom? The infinite love of God that Jesus wants to teach by example is surely the defining picture we get of him from Luke.

To return to the birth story, there is also a difference from Matthew in the genealogy. Matthew is affirming the Jewishness of Jesus and that Jews need not be afraid to follow him. Luke, writing for all the people, traces Jesus' ancestry back to Adam, the mythical first man, de-emphasizing the Jewish background in favor of the fact that Jesus has come for the sake of all humankind.

If Jesus is becoming a more universal figure in Luke, it is in John that we see him as the cosmic redeemer. This Gospel was the last to be written, sometime around the end of the first century. What we have seen traced so far begins with the sayings and deeds of Jesus, including his healing, with commands to follow a value system at odds with Roman and Greek culture and with the prevailing elites of his own race. Then, as what became the four Gospels began to be written, the authors paid more attention to the question, Who was this man? We can trace in the Gospels what the scholars call a budding Christology, until in John the life story of Jesus—his ethical commands, his healing—is subordinated to what is essentially a long sermon. There are only four separate healings recorded in John, as opposed to the frequent references both to specific healings and to his healing of the multitudes in the other Gospels. Jesus is presented more in terms of what traditional, or orthodox, Christians would call his divine status, and what in Christian Science is considered his Christly nature—his representation of God's perfect man. It is man's essential spiritual nature that is what offers him a full salvation. It is only in John that we are told that if we know the truth, it will make us free. That reference sounds like a call to understand the timeless Christ.

The Gospel is thought to have been written in Alexandria, one of the great centers of learning in the Roman Empire, and written for the Jews of the Diaspora. A generation had passed since the destruction of the Jewish temple, and John envisioned, instead of a restored Israel, a spiritual state.

Whoever wrote the Gospel of John, along with Paul's letters, established the basis for the complex Christian theology that evolved over the next four or five centuries. Paul himself did not attempt to write a life story of Jesus, nor appear to have been interested in the details of his mission. Yet one cannot tackle a subject like this and omit Paul. There is less emphasis in Paul on Jesus being divine than there is on Jesus' death and resurrection. It is Paul who writes in his earliest letters that "Christ died for our sins." Paul does refer to Jesus several times as the son of God, but he also says five times that we all may become the sons of God. Paul certainly picks up on the egalitarianism of Jesus, which Jesus demonstrated in eating with sinners, in healing those who were untouchable, and in treating women as equals. It is Paul who emphasizes that there is neither free nor slave, male nor female, etc., and in the few places where people have chewed some of his phrases to pieces to show that he hated women or some such thing, it is quite easy to see through such interpretations. It was Paul's vision of the universality of Christianity that caused his disagreement with Peter and the Jerusalem church over circumcision and dietary laws, and it was this universality that largely explained the rapid spread of Christianity.

How Jesus Viewed His Mission

Now I would like to turn for a few minutes to a discussion of how Jesus saw his own mission. This part of my talk owes much to a new book jointly written by Marcus Borg and N. T. Wright, entitled *The Meaning of Jesus*. Borg is a member of the Jesus Seminar and is what would probably be labeled a liberal Christian. He is certainly a scholar. Wright is dean of Lichfield Cathedral in England, and although both are Episcopalians, Wright speaks from what would be labeled an orthodox viewpoint. Their entire book is fascinating and challenging reading, as they take up eight topics about Jesus and politely debate them in alternating essays. What I want to turn to here is their interpretation of Jesus' mission.

Wright looks on Jesus as a figure entirely in the Jewish tradition. He knew that his people were looking for a savior, a messiah. Wright claims that "many, perhaps most, Jews longed for the day when they would not be ruled by the Roman emperor or even by the pseudo royal house of Herod but would have God alone for their sovereign." The kingdom of God phrase meant to them, he says, not a place where God ruled, but the *fact* that God ruled. So he begins by saying that Jesus was a first-century Jewish prophet announcing God's kingdom. Jesus "was telling his contemporaries that the kingdom was indeed breaking into history, *but that it did not look like what they had expected.*" It would not come about through violence or revolution, but rather through a moral transformation of the people themselves.

This is a view virtually identical to Crossan's concept of an ethical eschatology. Moreover, Jesus believed that this kingdom was "breaking in to Israel's history in and through his own presence and work." He welcomed all, including sinners, into this kingdom, and this angered his contemporaries. Let me quote a paragraph from Wright: "Ultimately, the challenge Jesus offered was the challenge to a crazy, subversive wisdom in which ordinary human wisdom, and conventional Jewish wisdom, would be stood on its head. To take up the cross and follow Jesus meant embracing Jesus' utterly risky vocation: to be the light of the world in a way the revolutionaries had never dreamed of. It was a call to follow Jesus into political danger and likely death, in the faith that by this means Israel's God would bring Israel through its present tribulations and out into the new day that would dawn." He warned of "dire consequences" if his summons to this kingdom was ignored.

Wright claims that Jesus' saying that the wedding guests do not fast while the bridegroom is with them "is not timeless teaching about religion or morality. It is a claim about eschatology. The time is fulfilled; the exile is over the bridegroom is at hand...."

Jesus recognized that his program clashed with the agendas of the temple elite. Wright says that Jesus saw his own community of followers as the replacement for the physical temple. Finally, he concludes that through his symbolic actions, such as in the temple, and "in cryptic and coded sayings, that he believed he was Israel's messiah, the one through whom God would accomplish his decisive purpose."

Wright has described Jesus in terms of his Jewishness. He has also accepted most of the events related in the Gospels as fact. Borg, in contrast, tries to talk about Jesus in cross-cultural terms. He writes as someone who is deeply involved in the evolution of the written text of the Gospels. Borg explains the reasons for his approach elsewhere in the book. He is a college professor and has found that a good way to lead into a discussion of Christianity is to use a cross-cultural approach, since there are so many similarities in some parts of the world's major religions. In this case, he describes Jesus as a "Spirit person." He only means by this someone who is in communication with God. This is essential to the rest of his explanation of Jesus' life, since having direct access to God, that is, a nonmediated relationship with him, means that God is immanent, right here, as well as transcendent. Foundational to the rest of his discussion of Jesus are three points: Jesus was a Jewish mystic, Jesus was fully aware of his Jewish traditions, and Jesus saw injustice firsthand. Now out of Jesus' being this "Spirit person" sprang his ability to heal, his so-called wisdom teaching, his social views, and his initiation of a community of followers.

The healing flowed from his sense of compassion, surely, but more important, it was a sign that the time for every kind of deliverance was at hand. For Jesus said, "If it is by the Spirit of God that I cast out demons, then the kingdom of God has come upon you." Moreover, healing was an affirmation of man's "immediacy of access to God."

Next, Jesus was a wisdom teacher, a teacher of an alternative way of living. Most of this teaching was in the form of short sayings or parables, and most scholars believe these parts of the Gospels go back to the very bedrock of Jesus. Borg writes, "The primary purpose...was to invite hearers into a different way of seeing—of seeing God, themselves, and life itself." And the sources of Jesus' views, says Borg, were the mystical experiences he had, his daily communion with God. That he had a new way of looking at life is seen in the many healings of blindness or his remarks about light. He had a different center to his life—instead of being centered on the conventional world, he was centered on the sacred. And the culmination of this new way of looking at things was a life centered on love, on the disappearance of the social boundaries and various distinctions that are merely the products of human society.

This resulted almost necessarily in the "social prophet" role. It was because he saw a new way of living that he was critical of a social system that rested on royal or aristocratic oppression of everyone else, critical of an economy in which those at the top wrung out everything they could from the peasant class, and critical of a religious system that legitimated the ruling class. He was also critical of wealth, even though Matthew, writing for wealthy Jewish converts, downplayed this element. And finally, because he spoke and acted with the authority of someone with a view of what God was demanding, he attracted an informal following, the beginning of the "Jesus movement."

Where Borg disagrees with N. T. Wright is in whether Jesus saw himself as the Messiah. Wright, as we saw, thinks that knowing Jewish tradition and expectations, Jesus could not have helped but see himself as the Messiah, even though he was reticent until the end to claim that title for himself. Borg prefers to call the pre-Easter Jesus a Jewish mystic, and the post-Easter Jesus the Christian Messiah. It is not a small difference for him, because he feels that if one sees Jesus primarily as the Messiah, that belief and other theological doctrines become the definition of a Christian. On the other hand, if one sees what Jesus said and did, as far as the reconstructed record can clarify his life, being his follower becomes a matter of having the kind of relationship to God that empowered the kind of life Jesus lived. It becomes a matter of what one knows of God, of the sacred life, instead of merely what one believes.

Healing

So as far as the current status of research on the historical Jesus, we see that the biblical texts, as well as some of the early ones that did not make it into the canon, develop an increasingly complex view of Jesus. What has not been specifically discussed are the healings of Jesus, and this may lead some to think that modern scholarship dismisses the healings. That is not the case at all, although different scholars give them different degrees of attention. Since the restoration of the practice of physical healing though prayer was the foundation stone of the new church Mrs. Eddy established, it is necessary to discuss what at least a few of today's scholars say on the subject in order to round out the current "picture" of Jesus.

First of all, Marcus Borg, who wrote *Meeting Jesus Again for the First Time*, definitely gives healing a major role in Jesus' life. He says, for instance, "He was a remarkable healer; more healing stories are told about him than about anybody else in the Jewish tradition." He also says, "Modern scholars generally accept that there is a historical core to the healing and exorcism stories, even though we may not be confident that any particular story is a detailed report of a specific incident."

Why was Jesus a healer? Because he was what Borg calls "a spirit person." This is the same as "holy man," but spirit person does away with the gender problem, and spirit conveys a meaning that holy does not. Holy generally means pious, says Borg, while the meaning he wants to convey is that of "a person to whom the sacred is an experiential reality." Spirit persons are those "who have vivid and frequent subjective experiences of another level or dimension of reality. Such persons become mediators of the sacred....They mediate the Spirit in various ways. Sometimes they speak the word or will of God. Sometimes they mediate the power of God, in the form of healings and/or exorcisms."

This other level of reality, the spiritual, is not off somewhere else. As William James, the psychologist/philosopher, explained it, "...we are separated from it only by filmy screens of consciousness. When those screens of consciousness momentarily drop away, the experience of Spirit occurs." To enter this consciousness, it's necessary to let the level of materiality in which we seem to live drop away. Thus the need for prayer and fasting. Jesus, we are told, often prayed all night long, and Borg comments that this was "presumably not because his prayer list had gotten exceptionally long." Like some other Jewish healers of his era, "It was said in the Jewish tradition that they would still their hearts before God before they could heal."

Then let us look at what Crossan has to say about miracles. He agrees that Jesus was a healer and an exorcist, and repeats Borg's mantra that no single healing may be fully historical. As for the nature miracles, such as walking on the water or feeding the multitudes, he notes that most of these stem from the early Church. It is very interesting to see how Crossan handles the explanation of the meaning of miracles, because although stated more intellectually, what he is saying is just about the same as what Borg said. That is, Jesus healed by drawing closer to God. Crossan says, "...even for believers and even within a theological framework, faith in an epiphanic God is not the same as faith in an episodic God. The former is a permanent divine presence periodically observed by believers. The latter is an absent presence periodically intervening for believers....To say, therefore, that the healings or exorcisms of Jesus are miracles does not mean for me that only Jesus could do such things but that in such events I see God at work in Jesus." That is, it's our own drawing closer in prayer, or thought, to a God who is right here, an ever-presence in our midst, that brings healing.

Then there is the Thomas Cahill book, *Desire of the Everlasting Hills*. Cahill acknowledges the problem so-called modern man has in acknowledging the miracles. He then goes on to discuss the weakness of the various attempts to explain them away, including the claim that Jesus was hoodwinking the multitudes, as he puts it. But listen to this: "A careful analysis of the texts of the Gospels, however, has convinced many scripture scholars that several, perhaps even a majority, of the basic miracle stories go back to the most primitive layer of the oral tradition—that is, to the testimony of the original eyewitnesses." He quotes John Meier, a professor who has done a multivolume study of the miracle stories, as follows: "The statement that Jesus acted as and was viewed as an exorcist and healer during his public ministry has as much historical corroboration as almost any other statement we can make about the Jesus of history."

Furthermore, Jesus' reply to John about whether he was the promised one, in which he recounts the healing of the blind and deaf and so on, occurs in identical language in both Matthew and Luke, which means that it comes from the Q source, which was probably written down at least a generation before the Gospels were written.

I decided to conclude this talk with the discussion of the healings for two reasons: first, because the reality of spiritual healing is well known to many or even most of you in this audience, and it is in a sense reassuring to hear modern scholarship accept the authenticity of so many of the healing events in Jesus' life that played a major role in shaping Mrs. Eddy's discussion of spiritual healing; second, because we should not be afraid of honest scholarship about the historical Jesus. We are in a period of intense interest in Jesus' life. The competition among scholars is intense, and I think that

that tends to prevent any scholarship from being taken seriously if it is undertaken primarily as an attempt to buttress the prevailing theological view of some group. Anything that draws us closer to the historical Jesus, as I believe this effort to lay out the time line of the writings about his life during the first century of our era does, can only serve in the end to make us think more deeply about what it means to be his disciple—his follower.

The Birth and Resurrection Stories

Two of the elements in the Gospel stories about Jesus gave me grave intellectual doubts for many years. Only with the perspective of an older person, and also with the time I took to read and think about the problem these elements gave me did I come to the conclusion I now have on the matter. These elements were the birth stories and the physical resurrection, neither one hardly a minor matter in the orthodox Christian story.

Mrs. Eddy accepted them both as literally true, and one reason I gave myself for not doubting the Bible story was her metaphysical interpretation of each. In the case of the virgin birth, the pure thought of Mary enabled her to bypass the normal route to pregnancy. Shortly after my mother-in-law married a famous endocrinologist in the early 1960s, he took me aside one evening and wanted to discuss the virgin birth. He knew the position Christian Science took regarding it (and was himself the son of a Methodist minister) and wanted to explain that it was simply fanciful. I had to agree that, of itself, it was indeed the stuff of fancy. However, if one had the faith imputed to Mary, it still seemed possible that this singular event could have occurred.

But look at the Bible narrative, or narratives. There are four of them. Two, Mark and John, do not even mention the circumstances of Jesus' birth. In Mark, the story begins with

Jesus' preaching and healing. John, written from a mystical standpoint (or in Christian Science terminology, from the standpoint of the Christ, the perfect man whom Jesus represented), has even less interest in the physical circumstances. As for Matthew and Luke, from which we get our wonderful Christmas stories of the angel's visitation, the shepherds in the fields, and the three Magi coming with gifts, the accounts are clearly contradictory. And from the standpoint of developing Christian theology fifty years after the time of Jesus, they all have a special purpose in the telling. The gifts of the wise men, for instance—gold, frankincense, and myrrh—are three ways of establishing the authority of Jesus' life—an earthly king, a religious leader, and a sacrificial death. If these stories helped to establish the claims that the young Jesus movement made on the world, so be it, but they were no longer any part of what held me to the Christian story. Nor would I want to argue about them with someone to whom they are still part of the "proof" of Jesus' mission. (The same can be said for the isolated verses of so-called "proof text" in the Hebrew Scriptures, which were thoroughly scanned by the Gospel writers for the purpose, again, of establishing a biblical prediction of Jesus' coming.)

As for the resurrection, I told you early in this talk that a mainline Congregational minister had sown the seeds of disbelief in that one Easter Sunday. It certainly had not lessened his commitment to Christianity. Again, I had Mrs. Eddy's metaphysics to maintain my belief in this for the better part of my adult life. It was Jesus' understanding of his true spiritual identity, the Christ, that could not be injured or destroyed, that allowed him to come through the ordeal of the crucifixion a victor.

I was aware that Harper's Bible Dictionary has another explanation. The earliest record concerning Jesus' resurrection, comes in I Corinthians, chapter fifteen, and the Harper's entry notes that "faith in the resurrection was based not on the empty tomb but on the appearances of the Lord." And these appearances need to be understood in terms that the thought of religious persons two millennia ago would have understood them—they were "visionary experiences," "disclosures from the transcendental realm."

What eventually made me rethink my concept of the resurrection, however, was not Harper's Dictionary. It came about at the time I was writing my book, *The New Birth of Christianity*. I had given permission to the Board of Directors of The First Church of Christ, Scientist, whose permission I would need in turn for quotations from Mrs. Eddy's writings or for their possible interest in selling the book when it was published, to look at my manuscript. One of the Directors, after reading the manuscript, told me that under no circumstances should I say that Jesus had actually died during the crucifixion experience. This was not entirely a new interpretation, as I had heard from my own teacher in Christian Science that there was a small minority of Christian Science teachers who taught this interpretation.

This view apparently originated with a doctor (Dr. Tutt) in Kansas City who became a Christian Science practitioner and then a teacher early in the twentieth century. He taught classes for close to forty years, and I had even heard him give a testimony in The Mother Church in the late 1940s, when I was a student at Harvard. His view was that, had Jesus been utterly dead, there would have been no one to "work," or pray, for his resurrection. This person believed the story of Jesus' raising Lazarus from the dead, because it was Jesus who prayed for Lazarus, Jesus who knew that Lazarus's life could not be destroyed by death. But in the case of Jesus, who would have intervened with prayer? We would be left only with a God (thinking here of God as another person) who could intervene.

The comments Mrs. Eddy makes about Jesus' crucifixion can be interpreted two ways. A literal reading of the textbook could lead to either opinion—was he dead or not? She says, for instance, that Jesus was "alive in the tomb." Well, what was alive? I talked with one teacher who had become a teacher through the instruction of another teacher who came from this tradition, and she said her understanding was that he was in a kind of semi-coma, but able to pray for himself. The fact for me remained, however, that if he was dead, he was dead! And this was what I had learned in my instruction in Christian Science.

However, if one simply looks at the Gospel stories, there seems ample evidence from Jesus' own words that he did not anticipate a physical resurrection. When Judas assailed Jesus for letting Mary, the sister of Martha, anoint him with oil, Jesus answered that she did it in preparation for his own burial. More well-known is his phrase "Greater love hath no man than this, that a man lay down his life for his friends." Does laying down one's life mean just that? And then on the cross, he said to one of the others being crucified, "Today you shall be with me in paradise."

Finally, there is Paul's own account of meeting Jesus on the road to Damascus. After discussing the other appearances of Jesus after the resurrection, he says that Jesus appeared to him last. No one would suggest that this was anything other than a subjective appearing; yet Paul puts it in the same category as the other appearances. In other words, it seems to me that the many Bible stories of Jesus' appearance after the crucifixion are all stories of appearances. They tell us that Jesus' presence came to each of his followers in the manner that *they needed* to carry on.

Clearing away what now seem to me to be literal interpretations of what even at the time of their telling may have been recognized as metaphors has not in any way weakened my practice as a Christian or as a Christian Scientist. Whether Mrs. Eddy, were she alive today, would reach these same conclusions, I do not know. What I do know is that I reached an honest conclusion to the matter in my own thought and that it has not weakened my allegiance to what I regard as the primary element that is unique to Christian Science—the spiritual power that can come to one as he acknowledges and tries to practice the oneness with God that Jesus proclaimed.

Considering the previous chapter on God and this one on Jesus may yield an explanation of why many Christians, especially in what is called the evangelical wing of the religion, may be confused when they use the name "Lord." Is it Jesus or God? Jesus as an individual we can all relate to. The more one considers the difficulty of defining in human language what one means by the word God, the easier it is to concentrate on what all Christians believe was his supreme manifestation—Christ Jesus. The important point for me, however, is that it is a consideration of Jesus' life that leads us to a knowledge of what God *does*. It is to God that we look for guidance on how to live—and in the terms of Christian Science, to the Christ, the perfect man of whom Jesus was the representative.

Chapter Six

THE HEBREW SCRIPTURES

The chapter you have just read, dealing with the meaning of the life of Jesus for Christians, is the subject of the New Testament. The Bible that Christians read, however, also contains what they call the Old Testament. The books in it are actually the Hebrew Scriptures, that part of the Bible that Christians share with Jews. Nothing should make Christians more aware of the fact that their religion is an offshoot, or development, of Judaism. Christians are generally familiar with the main characters of the Old Testament—Abraham, Isaac, Jacob, Joseph, Moses, David, and Solomon. But they tend to study those stories in small fragments, to apply the moral lessons they may contain for everyone.

You may recall that I quoted Emerson as saying that the Bible had no "epic integrity." By this I think he meant that it is not a single story such as is unfolded in Virgil's *Iliad* or Homer's *Odyssey*. But that claim is only partially correct. For the first two books of the Hebrew Scriptures are a saga of the development of Israel as a nation—from the legend of Abraham leaving his home in Ur (somewhere in the present country of Iraq), through the story of Joseph and his family settling in Eqypt, to the escape from Egypt led by Moses, and the sense of founding a new nation once they had crossed the Red Sea.

Of course, all the details of the story may not have happened exactly as they were written. For instance, there is no evidence of the Jews having escaped from Egypt, other than the Bible story itself. But the general drift of the story must be based on events that were told and retold until they solidified into the present story. In any case, the whole period from Abraham to Moses constitutes the epic on which the Jewish identity is framed. As a matter of simple historical interest, it is one that any educated person ought to be familiar with.

It is now almost twenty years since Allan Bloom, professor of social thought at the University of Chicago, wrote *The Closing of the American Mind.* In this book he lamented the state of American higher education, especially the lack of knowledge of the past that is needed if a society is to have any historical continuity.

In it, he mentioned among many other things the lack of knowledge of the biblical stories. He claimed that for students who lack any knowledge of what the vast amount of art that hangs on the walls of museums throughout the Western world or in the vaulted archways of cathedrals portrays, these pictures would be nothing more to them than studies in color. Yet, before literacy became widespread, most of the stories in the Bible were depicted in pictures, pictures that reminded the viewers of the story behind each work of art. It is the sharing of these common experiences—even when they do not resonate with one's own world view today—that builds an appreciation of the past and links human history in some kind of continuity.

Thomas Cahill has written several books on important turning points in human history. The whole series is called *The Hinges of History*, and seven books are planned. The second in the series, *The Gifts of the Jews*, is a short, very readable book in which he recounts what were for him the important elements in human thought that the Jewish patriarchs contributed to human civilization.

A book like this can do much to provide the kind of overview of the Hebrew Scriptures that prevents one from getting lost in the countless episodes of battles against various enemies. Christians are generally used to hearing an entire chapter of the Bible—or at least lengthy excerpts from a chapter—read at their church services. But such reading does little to explain the context in which these words were written down. And Christian Scientists study the Bible diligently when they read the weekly Lesson Sermon. But the excerpts they read are often even more concentrated— sometimes a single verse or two from a single chapter—in order to elucidate an idea. None of these uses of the Bible is wrong, but neither do they give one a sense of gratitude and, I think, awe at the fact that the Hebrew Scriptures is the early history of a small group of desert nomads who became a nation and then were under foreign rule until 1948. More important, it constitutes the story of how the concept of monotheism gradually emerged—the steps by which God was thought of as "their" God, then God of all the peoples of the earth; first a God who could be described and heard only in personal terms, and then finally a God who became the quiet voice everywhere present, speaking to all men, if they would listen.

To return to the Cahill book—in two instances I shall mention, he gives valuable insight into the historic roles played by Abraham and Moses that are often overlooked in teaching young people some of the details of their histories. Abraham came out of the Sumerian culture in what is now Iraq, the eastern part of the Middle East's fertile crescent. He lived in a culture that was essentially cyclical, that is, men saw the future as a mere repetition of the past. But Abraham, says Cahill, felt called by God to go out and search for something new. God, still not the *only* God, is sensed as a personal being who calls Abraham to begin, as it were, a new history. God says to Abraham, "Get thee out of thy country, and from thy kindred, and from thy father's house; unto a land that I will shew thee" (Gen.12:1). It is the beginning of a new kind of relationship with God. It is a relationship in which God directs man, and one in which history is no longer cyclical, but holds the possibility of progress.

The Abrahamic migration is believed to have taken place somewhere around the year 2000 BCE. Jumping many hundreds of years ahead, the story of Moses leading the children of Israel out of Egypt is supposed to have happened somewhere around 1200 BCE. Moses is the first biblical character after Abraham whom the Bible identifies as directly hearing the voice of God—the burning bush legend. Moses is a humble man and cannot believe that he is the one to lead his people to freedom. Yet he is eventually convinced that this is his God-given task, and after the trials his people go through in getting permission to leave, the crossing of the Red Sea takes place, an event of which Cahill rightly says, "This story of deliverance is the central event of the Hebrew Scriptures. In retrospect, we can see that all the wandering of the forefathers and foremothers and their growing intimacy with God have led up to this moment; and looking down the ages from this shore, we can see that everything that happens subsequently will be referred back to this moment of astonished triumph."

At the time of the burning bush, God revealed himself to Moses as the Great I Am, or I AM THAT I AM, or I WILL BE WHAT I WILL BE. Various scholars have translated the Hebrew words in different ways. The I WILL BE form somewhat correlates with Northrop Frye's definition of God as a verb, suggesting that God is active in human history. In every case, though, what is suggested is that, although the fullness of God is entirely beyond human comprehension, God is a Being to be listened to and obeyed.

After the Israelites have escaped from Egypt and begin their wandering in the desert, God again speaks to Moses in giving him the Ten Commandments. Cahill reminds us that no one has yet come up with a better set of rules. Even those who have given up on the concept of a theistic God find the rules for human morality simple and complete. When Moses first delivered the Commandments, they were most likely in the simplest imaginable form—the ones to do with human behavior, commands like "not kill."

Going beyond the time of Moses leading the Hebrews for forty years, the Bible does have a historical time line that one can follow. In fact, everything before the time of Moses belongs partly to the realm of legend and cannot be easily verified as history. But after the time of Moses and the judges, the Jews decide they want to have a king like other nations. So there are the stories of Saul, David, and Solomon, in the eleventh and tenth centuries BCE. David reigned for forty years, from 1010 BCE to 970 BCE. Solomon reigned for forty years after him. After the reign of Solomon, there were disputes among his sons, and the kingdom was split up into northern and southern kingdoms—Israel and Judah. There is sufficient historical material about other cultures and rulers of the time to corroborate the history in the Hebrew Scriptures from this period onward.

Many of the books in the Hebrew Scriptures are the writings of the prophets who came after the time of Solomon. Isaiah (actually two or perhaps three separate writers), Jeremiah, Ezekiel, and Daniel are generally classed as the major prophets. There are also twelve so-called minor prophets, minor only because their books are very slender volumes. However, two of the minor prophets were the first to appear on the scene after the splitting up of Israel.

In her book *The Prophets for the Common Reader*, Mary Ellen Chase begins by setting straight the misconception that any of these prophets were talking about events in the far-off future. They were reacting to what they saw as the evils of their own day and telling the people what would happen to them if they did not reform. She writes, "This mistaken idea of prediction by the prophets, of foretelling the future, existed early in the Christian church and is by no means absent from it today. It is seen in the quite erroneous notion that certain of them looked seven centuries beyond their own time and foresaw the coming of Jesus of Nazareth, which they foretold in those prophecies known as Messianic. To believe this is a simple distortion of historical truth. The great Hebrew prophets were without doubt precursors of Jesus....But they belonged to their own day, and their hopes for peace and order in their own world as proclaimed by certain of them had to do *with their world* and not with far distant future centuries of which they, of course, knew nothing."

The prophets' minds, she writes, "like all Hebrew minds, were not speculative so much as intuitive..." They did not have a developed theology; they conceived of God as creator of the universe, but most important, as a personal God who was never far from the humanity he had formed. She continues, "This idea of active participation in the daily affairs of men, this common life shared by God and His people, is emphasized by all the prophets, who in their concrete, personal metaphors see Him always as inseparable from the homely actions and happenings of daily life." This is one reason God is often referred to as "redeemer," since in Israel the redeemer was the family member who was responsible for the continuity of the family. But this God was a God who demanded absolute obedience from his people, and it was because the people had strayed so far from the basic teachings of their fathers that the prophets were warning them.

The first two, Amos and Hosea, writing in the eighth century BCE, warned the people of Israel that they would be punished for their soft and immoral ways. In particular, they stressed the community's responsibility to care for the unfortunate. Hosea, who had an unfaithful wife, also wrote in metaphorical terms of Israel's lack of faithfulness to God. Both prophets had it right: In 711 BCE the Northern Kingdom was destroyed, and the ten tribes of Israel that had constituted that kingdom were lost to history. The two tribes in the south, Judah and Simeon, continued until they were carried off to Babylon more than a century later.

Isaiah is the work of at least two writers, possibly three. The first Isaiah, of Jerusalem, wrote for an extended period, from about 740 BCE to 700 BCE. His writing is considered some of the most beautiful in the Hebrew Scriptures and is quoted more than any other book with the exception of the Psalms. His warnings were meant for the Kingdom of Judah, which was eventually attacked in 701 BCE. The second Isaiah wrote more than one hundred fifty years later and was reacting to the destruction of the Temple in Jerusalem and the enforced movement of the Jews from Judah to Babylon. In the interval, Jeremiah had prophesied the destruction of the Temple and of Jerusalem, which is what actually happened in 587 BCE when Nebuchadnezzar attacked the city. Jeremiah lived through it all, and part of his "book" is written to the Jewish exiles in Babylon.

While Isaiah may be the most beautiful in language of the prophets, Chase finds Jeremiah the most human. In an extended passage about him, she writes, "Many students and readers of Jeremiah have seen in him not so much a teacher of religious truths, not so much a prophet, as a great human personality. To them he symbolizes the awakened mind of man, often doubting, seldom free from fear, yet dead and useless without devotion, even dedication to a Power beyond itself which alone gives meaning to human life....His unanswered and unanswerable questions becomes their own and he himself not only the most compassionate and companionable of the prophets, but in a very real sense the symbol and the image of every man in his restless, never-ending search after 'the things of God.'"

When did the Hebrew Scriptures come into being? That is, when did these various sections we call books get written down? Much of the history of the Jews, as recorded in Joshua, Judges, Samuel, and Kings, was put together in the latter part of the seventh century BCE, that is, the early 600s BCE, before the exile in Babylon. What is called the Torah, the first five books of the Bible, was pieced together by scholars from perhaps four different sources during or shortly after the period of the Babylonian exile, which would have been a century later. The Psalms, at least those attributed to David and his period, belong to an earlier time, 900 BCE or so. Scholars presently believe, however, that the composition of most of the Psalms belongs to the period after the exile, which formally ended in 538 BCE. I have left out a few of the other books, but my purpose in getting into even this much detail is to give some idea of the process by which legend and history became interwoven in the final text. These were the books that were known to Jesus, and he can be presumed to have been intimately acquainted with the history of his own people and with the warnings of the prophets.

This is history that is well known to Jews. It should also be a part of every Christian's heritage, since it all belongs to the story that Christians find completed in the life of Christ Jesus (whether or not they subscribe to the prophetic analogies that abound in Matthew). They are the beginnings and development of the story of the concept of God in human history. From the tribal gods of the Sumerians and other kingdoms of the time, to a God that Abraham believed was directing him, to the God of Moses who revealed the moral code, to a God who was not just the God of the Israelites, but of the universe, from a God who could seem more like a tyrant to one who was demanding, but also loving and forgiving—all of these concepts are there and not always in a neat time line, as many of the concepts that are somewhat contradictory could have been believed and acted on at the same time. But the theme that runs through them all is that God is supreme and must be obeyed and understood, as much as human thought can take in the immensity of infinity. Chase writes that Hosea wrote of understanding God in the manner in which a man knows a woman: He was saying one must have intimate communion with God. When he says of God, "My people are destroyed for lack of knowledge," it is this close communion that He means, not theoretical brain knowledge.

And it was in the exile in Babylon that a further step occurred in the development of the Jews' concept of God. Their temple had been destroyed; they were uprooted from their homes. In seventy years they were allowed to return, but not all of them did. The Jewish Diaspora had begun and would continue. Without a national identity, what did they have? What would hold them together and give them the cohesive identity they have maintained into modern times? Cahill suggests that the exile experience was the beginning of the internalizing of religion, of man's concept of God. "There was in every human being an 'inside,' which the Jews had never steadily adverted to before. Could God possibly mean that each of them was to be a king, a prophet, a priest in his own right?" He continues, "Could it be that this inside—where the 'still, small voice' that spoke to Elijah resided—was the real Temple of God?" Such thoughts would not have been universal, but for some Jews they must have been the start of the internalization of God that I spoke of in Chapter Three.

Jewish tradition does not emphasize the creation stories in the first few chapters of Genesis as much as Christian theology does. While the Jews certainly believed that man sinned, and they had a very realistic sense of evil, they did not take on the burden of original sin coming from Adam that St. Augustine placed on Christians many centuries later.

In fact, the Jews were more concerned with obeying what was revealed to them of God's laws, of God's demand on them, than they were with a system of theology. Scholars today believe that the Adamic story, in the second chapter of Genesis, predates the first chapter, in which God creates a perfect universe and pronounces himself satisfied with what he has created. (This is the basis for Mrs. Eddy's sense of a perfect spiritual universe that has remained intact.) The first chapter, ending with God's resting on the seventh day, is believed to be a priestly version and perhaps stems from the Jews' need to emphasize the Sabbath as the vehicle for holding them together after the Temple in Jerusalem had been destroyed.

In the Western, Judeo-Christian tradition, even nonreligious individuals should be familiar with the Hebrew Scriptures. They are the written record of the Jews' search for God, for meaning in what was for them a tempestuous existence (and what for us today may at times be just as stormy). But this claim for the Old Testament may raise another question: Why should we not be just as familiar with the teachings of the Koran or the Upanishads, the last section of the Veda, the Hindu holy scriptures? Perhaps in an ideal world we should be. However, if most of the younger generation knows as little as it seems to know about the Old Testament, it is asking too much to expect them to venture further into the religious scriptures of the rest of mankind.

Furthermore, scriptures cannot just be read. Even an understanding of much of the Old Testament requires that the reader try to reenter the world of two thousand and more years ago and feel the emotion that gripped these writers in the times they lived in. It would be much more difficult to enter the world of the Hindus, or to understand the plight of the desert nomads turning to the Koran for instruction. Only a relatively small number of scholars over the years has been able to enter the mental world of another culture in a manner that would enable them to understand the mind-set, the world outlook, of those who benefited from those scriptures. At the same time, however, that leaves no excuse for denigrating the value of other religious systems and their own scriptures—scriptures that have nourished the people of other cultures over longer periods of time than we have had the Hebrew Scriptures and the New Testament.

Chapter Seven

WILLIAM JAMES

Emerson was important to me as a young man. I have mentioned that his call for individual thinking, for independence, resonated with me as a young adult. Of course it still does, but it was particularly valuable at that time in my life. Emerson also represented the mood of early nineteenth-century America, and the general optimism of at least his early and middle years fit well with the mood of an optimistic nation undergoing growth pains and expansion.

William James stands in a similar position vis-a-vis late nineteenth-century America. He seems larger-than-life when one considers the various aspects of his career. His grandfather had struck it rich as one of the builders of the Erie Canal. His father, William Sr., traveled widely in Europe, and after a nervous breakdown, he was helped by turning to the religious philosophy of Swedenborg. The James children were raised largely in New York City, in what at the time would have been considered an extremely liberal intellectual atmosphere. William's brother Henry became the famous novelist. William himself went to Harvard, received his M.D. in 1869, and in 1872 became a professor of physiology there.

That is only the beginning. James's interests were universal from the start. He devoured philosophy. He was a naturalist. He was one of the great pioneers in psychology and took a decade, from 1880 to 1890, to produce his text, *Principles of Psychology*. He had been raised without formal religious belief (William Sr. had not bestowed his Swedenborgian beliefs on the sons). However, his psychological studies of various states of mind carried him to the realm of religion, and his book *The Varieties of Religious Experience*, the written version of his 1901-02 Edinburgh lectures, remains an American classic. He also was closely associated with the philosophical movement of pragmatism. Although not its actual founder, he gave it its name and, in the public mind, remains its most understandable exponent. And toward the end of his life he promoted the concept of pluralistic universes. Unlike most philosophers looking for a system into which they could fit all human experience, James answered, Why? But it is to *The Varieties of Religious Experience* that we turn here.

James was not interested in religious doctrines or dogma, but in the lives of people who were religious. The Edinburgh lectures were devoted to a discussion of various types of religious experience—the once-born, the twice-born, the mystics, the saints, and so on. But the two concluding chapters of his book say almost all of the things I would like to leave with you, only in rather stuffy academic language and certainly not religious language. Let us look first at how he summed up his study of religious experience and then see how parts of it fit with Christianity, particularly with Christian Science.

First of all, James found a common thread in the experience of all the religious people he studied or read about. There was, first, what he called an "uneasiness," and second, a "solution." "The uneasiness," he said, "reduced to its simplest terms, is a sense that there is *something wrong about us* as we naturally stand. The solution is a sense that we *are saved from wrongness* by making proper connection with the higher powers."

We sense that there is a better person within us, "even though it may be but a most helpless germ." Man becomes conscious, he said, "that this higher part is conterminous and continuous with a MORE of the same quality, which is operative in the universe outside of him, and which he can keep in working touch with, and in a fashion get on board of and save himself when all his lower being has gone to pieces in the wreck." And it is no surprise that this MORE is usually called God by religious people.

It does not matter to James whether this X factor, which we will call God, is infinite or not, only that it is something besides ourselves. That is the scientist in James at work, not claiming more than he needs to in order to make his case.

James also discusses whether this God does a "retail business" or only "wholesale." He cannot agree with many of his generation's thinkers that God is a cosmic force operating in all the laws of the universe, but certainly not one that can be appealed to on an individual basis. He finds the "wholesale God" meaningless in terms of individual lives. "In spite of the appeal which this impersonality of the scientific attitude makes to a certain magnanimity of temper, I believe it to be shallow...so long as we deal with the cosmic and general, we deal only with the symbols of reality, but as soon as we deal with private and personal phenomena as such, we deal with realities in the completest sense of the term." Our own reality is the only thing we actually know, and it is because religion occupies us with our personal destinies that it will always be a part of the human scene, he argues.

Those who do find this connection with another power, with something outside of themselves, share several views in common; he says "that the visible world is part of a more spiritual universe from which it draws its chief significance; that union or harmonious relation with that higher universe is our true end; that prayer with the spirit thereof—be that spirit "God" or "law"—is a process wherein *work is really done* [my italics], and spiritual energy flows in and produces effects, psychological or material, within the phenomenal world." He says this religious feeling, or impulse, also gives a new zest to life and usually involves "a preponderance of loving affections."

James himself was not a religious man. He had not had any of the religious experiences of which he writes so positively. He certainly believed them to be true. He also goes on to say that it is one thing to write about religion, but another to actively practice it. That is why he had little use for doctrine as such. He found that every organized religion had some doctrinal beliefs, but that the practices of the truly religious in every faith had much in common. But practice was necessary to make any progress in a religious sense. He said it was one thing to write about the state of drunkenness, and another to be drunk. "If we believe any of this, we have to LIVE it," he wrote. "If religion be a function by which either God's cause or man's cause is to be really advanced, then he who lives the life of it, however narrowly, is a better servant than he who merely knows about it."

As a psychologist, he thought that he had found "the mediating term" required to explain this belief in God. That term was the subconscious self, an entity just beginning to be explored by psychologists at that time. "Apart from all religious considerations, there is actually and literally more life in our total soul than we are at any time aware of."

When we commune with or, in religious terms, pray to this other self, "work is actually done upon our finite personality, for we are turned into new men, and consequences in the way of conduct follow in the natural world upon our regenerative change. But that which produces effects within another reality must be termed a reality itself, so I feel as if we had *no philosophic excuse for calling the unseen or mystical world unreal* [my italics].

In today's world, in which neuroscience is so much more advanced, I am sure there are critics who consider James's views to be simply "woolly." James might agree. On the other hand, he was venturing into an area that he probably believed would remain outside the boundaries of the five senses and human rationality. He concluded his own personal statement of belief with these sentences: "Humbug is humbug, even though it bear the scientific name, and the total expression of human experience, as I view it objectively, invincibly urges me beyond the narrow 'scientific' bounds. Assuredly, the real world is of a different temperament—more intricately built than physical science allows."

It is obvious that some of this resonates with the religious views of Christians. Whether the vague notion of this other power would be enough to satisfy most is another question. If it is only in the subconscious, the question would be, Do we share the same subconscious? Is there really anything out there besides us lone individuals? But does "out there" have to be in space? Can it not be that the inner space we all share is shaped and governed by the same laws, and that this is what God is?

Moreover, if you look back to what I wrote about a few of the mystics of the Middle Ages, you will remember that many of them felt it was wrong to try to put God into words. There was an ineffable quality about God that will forever defy definition. What the mystics found more important was what God *does*, or what God *requires*. If one can get beyond thinking of God as a thing, or even as the Supreme Being—but perhaps as Being itself—that is more important than a verbal definition. And many of the mystics were convinced that they had had a direct experience of God.

At the time James delivered the Edinburgh lectures (1901-02), Christian Science was undergoing rapid growth in America. Some of this growth could be attributed to a reaction against both the old-style evangelistic type of preaching and the more liberal Protestant theology that was gaining popularity. But the largest part of the movement's growth had to be attributed to the physical healing and the impressive results that were being reported. James was not unaware of this, and in the lectures he spoke specifically of Christian Science a few times and several times lumped it in with the wider movement of what he called mind-cure.

"The plain fact," he said, "remains that the spread of the movement has been due to practical fruits, and the extremely practical turn of character of the American people has never been better shown than by the fact that this, their only decidedly original contribution to the systematic philosophy of life, should be so intimately knit up with concrete therapeutics."

How did he account for this? Partly by referring to "the fundamental pillar...of all religious experience, the fact that man has a dual nature, and is connected with two spheres of thought, a shallower and a profounder sphere, in either of which he may learn to live more habitually." As a psychologist, he was familiar with current theories about the subconscious, the belief that from the depths of consciousness one could become aware of realities that were hidden from ordinary consciousness. But he also recognized that this had similarities to religious belief.

He maintained that it was "impossible...not to class mind-cure as primarily a religious movement, its doctrine of the oneness of our life with God's life is in fact quite indistinguishable from an interpretation of Christ's message which in these very Gifford lectures has been defended by some of your very ablest Scottish religious philosophers."

He concluded that this wide movement of mental healing had "dignity and importance. We have seen it to be a genuine religion, and no mere silly appeal to imagination to cure disease; we have seen its method of experimental verification to be not unlike the method of all science; and now here we find mind-cure as the champion of a perfectly definite conception *of* the metaphysical structure of the world."

James himself did not accept this metaphysical structure, by which I think he is alluding to the primacy of spiritual reality, the kingdom of heaven, if you will. But he would not close his eyes to its results. In the last book he published before his death in 1910, *A Pluralistic Universe*, he honed his theme that there could be more than one reality. Ever skeptical both of grand systems of metaphysics and of the claims of physical science that it alone possessed the "grand answers," he found no difficulty in mentally picturing several kinds of reality, each of which served a particular purpose. And in one sense that is the everyday world in which we all do our business.

In the terminology of Christian Science, this better self that we become conscious of is simply the Christ, the perfect man that Jesus represented in his life work. We all are God's children and we all have the Christ-identity as our true identity if we only claim it and live it. Furthermore, it seems to me that Christian Science handles the question of the "wholesale" versus the "retail" God. God is in one sense the universal lawgiver—that is the wholesale part. But as individuals we have to learn to identify ourselves with the Christ, with our direct, individual connection as God's perfect sons and daughters. Without the knowledge of this connection, of our true spiritual heritage, we cannot claim it. It is in the claiming of it that we have individual healing experiences, whether bodily or of any other kind of difficulty, that God becomes manifest as the "retail" God. Thus there is no real contradiction in using both terms to describe God.

The most impressive thing he wrote in this regard, being a nonreligious man, was to say that one had to practice whatever he thought he knew about this connection if it was to mean anything practical in his life. And it is with this tag line in mind that I approach the life of a twentieth-century Christian martyr in the next chapter.

Chapter Eight

DIETRICH BONHOEFFER

William James had little interest in religious belief as such. What fascinated him as a psychologist and philosopher was the *fact* of religious experience. As the previous chapter has shown, he had the highest regard for the individual who carried out whatever conviction lay at the core of his thought into concrete action.

In thinking about the many persons who have lived their lives according to their deepest religious convictions, Dietrich Bonhoeffer, a German Protestant theologian, has come to my thought. Many aspects of his life can be admired, although admire is too timid a word for the sacrifice that Bonhoeffer made for his fellow countrymen. Bonhoeffer's life also provides an excellent example of the ways in which one's own human experience transforms him. Bonhoeffer was a convinced pacifist for part of his life; yet in joining in the conspiracy against Hitler he took up arms as surely as if he had been a soldier on the Russian front. His life experience also transformed his religious views. Since these were expressed in brief letters written in prison, they are not fully articulated, and they are not the focus of what I am writing about here. At the least, though, they show both a continuity to his religious thought and a major change in its emphasis, thus proving another point: that the seeker after God does not stand in a static position.

Bonhoeffer was born in 1906. Although his great-grandfather had been a noted church historian, the present generation of the family were only nominally religious. His father was a neurologist and psychiatrist at the University of

Berlin. Bonhoeffer's interest in religion may have been a way of asserting his individuality within the family. In any case, he studied theology in Tubingen and Berlin and became acquainted with the greatest German theologians of the time. He was attracted to the neo-orthodoxy of Karl Barth and was later very warmly regarded by Barth. But from the start, he maintained his distance in developing his theological views.

In 1928 the young Dietrich accepted a position as the assistant in a German church in Barcelona. He came straight from academe in Berlin, and he was thrown into the lives of real people. He wrote in one letter that "the ground from under our feet, or rather the bourgeois rug from under our feet, has been pulled away and now it is a question of seeking the solid ground on which we stand." He found the church for the most part unable to meet people's needs. One of his editors writes that the papers he wrote at this period contain "hints of his later bitter indictment of the church for its having buried Jesus in a repelling heap of religiosity." In one of his sermons while he was in Spain, he said, "God wanders among us in human form, speaking to us in those who cross our path, be they stranger, beggar, sick, or even in those nearest to us in everyday life, becoming Christ's demand on our faith in him." He became convinced that only by working in community could a Christian fulfill Jesus' demands. He felt that the church, "in it power-hungry appropriation of revelation through doctrine, psychic experience, or institution, had tried to reduce God to itself."

In 1930 Bonhoeffer had the opportunity to study for a year on a grant at Union Theological Seminary in New York. He did not think that Americans had a very deep understanding of theology and did not expect to get much of substance from the Union experience. But the year did have a substantial effect on his developing social views. Reinhold Niebuhr, one of the American theological greats of the time (I used to hear him preach on occasion at Harvard during the late 1940s, and my Catholic roommate would ask me if Niebuhr had decided yet whether he believed in God!) probably felt that Bonhoeffer was too steeped in a theoretical Christianity, for in critiquing one of his student's papers he wrote, "In making grace as transcendent as you do, I don't see how you can ascribe any ethical significance to it. Obedience to God's will may be a religious experience but it is not an ethical one until it issues in actions which can be socially valued..."

Bonhoeffer was also introduced to the black churches in Harlem and to the racial and economic injustice the blacks suffered. He loved the black gospel music and took it home with him when he returned to Germany. In New York, his sense of what it meant to be a Christian was challenged by seeing the plight of the poor and the treatment of the blacks, and by rubbing shoulders with the likes of Niebuhr.

Back in Berlin, he became for a short time a popular university lecturer. But the rise of Hitler in the next year brought new challenges to the Lutheran (Evangelische) Church in Germany, and Bonhoeffer became involved in ecclesiastical opposition to the takeover of the church by the so-called "German Christians," those pastors who submitted to the increasing demands of the Nazi regime. Those ministers who did not go along with the German Christians held a series of meetings, called synods, at which they attempted to draft resolutions of opposition. The results were never as strong as Bonhoeffer urged, and in particular, they dodged the issue of the Jewish question. Bonhoeffer himself still apparently held to the old theological view (one that Luther strongly held) that the Jews were responsible for Jesus' death, but he also felt that no nation could take it upon itself to punish the Jews.

In the fall of 1933, he had the chance to take over a German parish in London. Thinking that he might have more influence there and could be out of the limelight for a while, he went to London. This was the beginning of an international experience that gave him contacts that would later be helpful in his work in the anti-Nazi underground as an employee of the Abwehr (Military Intelligence Service). However, this was certainly not in his thought at the time.

During these years in the mid-1930s, he was also a confirmed pacifist. This had been his position at least since his days as a post-graduate student in New York; he took to heart Jesus' beatitude, "Blessed are the peacemakers..." At one point during his year in New York, he and a fellow student from France had taken a trip to Mexico, where they both spoke as pacifists. Those they addressed were particularly impressed to see a Frenchman and a German agreeing as friends, just ten years after the First World War.

In 1935 some of the leaders of the Confessing Church decided to start a seminary of their own, and Bonhoeffer was asked to come back and be its leader. The group met at an old estate in Finsterwalde from the spring of 1935 until the Gestapo closed it down in October 1937. Here Bonhoeffer put into practice some of the new concepts he had. In many respects, the seminary was run less as we would think of a graduate school and more like a monastery. In fact, there was some criticism that he made it too Catholic. But he introduced daily group prayers, daily meditation, and so on in order to establish the value of certain practices as a normal part of one's religious life. At first, many of the seminarians did not know what to do with the meditation time; some even slept.

The year 1938 saw the noose tightening ever further around the necks of the Confessing Christians. After the Anschluss, the annexation of Austria, in the spring of 1938, all the ministers were required to take an oath of loyalty to Hitler. The Synod of the Confessing Church refused to take a stand against the oath, leaving that up to individual pastors. Bonhoeffer saw this as a serious weakening of any kind of unity within the remnant of faithful pastors. Then, after Kristallnacht in November, when synagogues and Jewish-owned stores were attacked, and the church as a united organization did not even protest, he felt still more desperate. Moreover, he knew that his age group would soon be called up for military service. When asked by his own cohort what he would do if he were called, he responded, after a long silence, that he hoped he would have the courage to refuse to go. (This could mean the death sentence.)

At the same time, he became aware that his brother-in-law, Hans von Dohnanyi, was involved in some scheme to topple Hitler. Because of the authoritarian history of the Germans (they had had no real experience with democracy except for the miserable decade of the Weimar Republic, 1919 to 1933), he knew that Hitler could be overthrown only by some kind of action from the top. But to join in any action against Hitler could mean certain death; moreover, he had his commitment to pacifism to consider. In a videotape made by his sister, von Dohnanyi's widow, in the early 1980s, she says in a very emotional statement that she spoke to him at the time and said in effect, What is it with you Christians? You won't kill but you want someone else to do the killing for you?

So, with this as background, it may have come with some relief to Bonhoeffer that, on his own initiative, he was able to negotiate an "invitation" to come to America again. Before he left in the spring of 1939, he talked with the general secretary of the World Council of Churches, who happened to be in London. According to the general secretary, Visser 't Hooft, "he spoke in a way that was remarkably free from illusions, and sometimes almost clairvoyant, about the coming war, which would start soon...Had not the time come to refuse to serve a government that was heading straight for war and breaking all the Commandments?" At any rate, the opportunity in America might give him time to sort out his thoughts and chart a future course of action.

Arrival in America had a reverse effect. He knew at once that he had made a mistake. He was right about what was going on in Germany, but as a German he felt he could not accept a safe berth in America while he knew others were and would be suffering. He stayed in America less than a month, sailed back to Germany in early July, and wrote these memorable words to Reinhold Niebuhr, words that in one sense sealed his own ultimate murder: "I have made a mistake in coming to America. I must live through this difficult period of our national history with the Christian people of Germany. I will have no right to participate in the reconstruction of German life in Germany after the war if I do not share the trials of this time with my people...Christians in Germany will face the terrible alternative of either willing the defeat of their nation in order that Christian civilization may survive, or willing the victory of their nation and thereby destroying our civilization. I know which of these alternatives I must choose; but I cannot make that choice in security."

The noose tightened still further around Bonhoeffer once he had returned. He was forbidden to teach any theology courses. Then, after Hitler's invasion of Poland in September 1939, he was banned from speaking in public and ordered to report to the police on a regular basis. At this time, his brother-in-law intervened, and seemingly miraculously got him assigned to the Abwehr, on the grounds that his ministerial travels were a good cover for intelligence work he could be assigned to carry out. Since the core of the plot against Hitler was in the Abwehr, this placed him in the spot where he could contribute the most to what he felt had to be done—to bring down the regime. And to get him away from the prying eyes of the Gestapo in Berlin, they had him assigned to live at the Benedictine Abbey in Ettal, near Munich. But the Gestapo maintained its suspicions and had been listening to the phones of both Bonhoeffer and von Dohnanyi. After two failed attempts on Hitler's life early in 1943, both men, as well as several others, were arrested.

The two years that follow reveal the depth of Bonhoeffer, the genuineness of his religious convictions, which sustained him as well as fellow prisoners for the next two years, and the continuing evolution of his religious thought. Although it is difficult to understand exactly where he was going in his thinking, he would undoubtedly have had a profound—and unsettling—effect on the Evangelische church had he survived the war. He had already published two books in the 1930s that established him as a leading thinker in the field, *The Cost of Discipleship* and *Life Together*.

Just before his arrest, he wrote a long letter meant for his immediate family called *After Ten Years*. In it he talked about the lessons he had learned during this most difficult decade for any civilized human being. The start of this epistle is what is relevant here, for it bears on his deportment during the two years that would follow his arrest. "Ten years is a long time in anyone's life," he began. "As time is the most valuable thing that we have, because it is the most irrevocable, the thought of any lost time in which we have failed to live a full human life, gain experience, learn, create, enjoy, and suffer; it is time that has not been filled up, but left empty. These last years have certainly not been like that. Our losses have been great and immeasurable, but time has not been lost."

Nor would time be lost in prison. After he had gained the goodwill of some of the prison guards, he was allowed a fairly normal correspondence. He had, of course, to refrain from any reference to the conspiracy. One of the anomalies of the Nazi period was the lack of coordination, at times, between various parts of the dictatorship, which allowed for the conspiracy to exist for as long as it did. In one bizarre incident, just before the plot against Hitler on July 20, 1944, his uncle, Paul von Hase, who was the Commandant of Berlin, visited him in prison and brought with him four bottles of champagne. Less than two months later, the discovery of von Hase's collaboration with the conspirators resulted in his being hanged with piano wire. The hanging was filmed for Hitler's evening enjoyment.

Other than family letters to his family, most of the rest of his correspondence was with his ministerial friends and concerned his evolving views of Christianity. He writes at some points of "religionless Christianity." Echoing some of the same things that A. N. Wilson says in *God's Funeral,* he notes that mankind in general seems to be getting along quite well without the concept of God. Consider this: "What is bothering me incessantly is the question what Christianity really is, or indeed who Christ really is, for us today. The time when people could be told anything by means of words, whether theological or pious, is over, and so is the time of inwardness and conscience—and that means the time of religion in general. We are moving toward a completely religionless time; people as they are now simply cannot be religious anymore."

I do not believe that any of his thoughts from prison were his final thoughts. These were tentative feelings he was testing, and no one knows for sure where he might have come out. He certainly did not foresee the end of religion, as is obvious in the thoughts he wrote toward the end of his prison life. He said that one could no longer ask the question, What *must* I believe? That had become irrelevant. Controversies between the sects, even with the Catholics, were no longer relevant. He also criticized Karl Barth, whom he had admired, for saying one must simply stand behind "the faith of the Church." Nothing mattered anymore, he said, except "the duty of being honest with ourselves."

As for what kind of church he envisioned, it would appear that it would have much less to do with traditional Christian doctrine. He no longer wanted a state-supported church, but one (as in America) supported by each congregation. "It must tell men of every calling what it means to live in Christ, to exist for others. In particular, our own Church will have to take the field against the vices of *hubris*, power-worship, envy, and humbug, as the roots of all evil. It will have to speak of moderation, purity, trust, loyalty, constancy, patience, discipline, humility, contentment, and modesty. It must not under-estimate the importance of human example...it is not abstract argument, but example, that gives its words emphasis and power."

Bonhoeffer's example in prison was a demonstration of the grace that he felt he received from God each day. One need not understand or even agree with the intricacies of his Lutheran background or its particular emphases to appreciate what it activated within him. A British secret agent, who had been a prisoner of the Gestapo since 1939, was with him toward the end, and he wrote of Bonhoeffer, "He always seemed to diffuse an atmosphere of happiness, of joy in every smallest event in life; and a deep gratitude for the mere fact that he was alive....He was one of the very few men I have ever met *to whom his God was real and ever close to him.*"

Yet to me, knowing that he must have wondered at times, as Job did, why all this had come to him makes him seem even more human. In a poem he wrote toward the end, which he called *Who Am I?*, he juxtaposed the two Bonhoeffers within him. In one stanza, for instance, he says, "Who am I? They often tell me I would talk to my warders freely and friendly and clearly, as though it were mine to command." In another stanza he shows his other self: "Or am I only what I know of myself; restless and longing and sick, like a bird in a cage, struggling for breath, as though hands were compressing my throat." He finds resolution in his faith: "Who am I? They mock me, these lonely questions of mine. Whoever I am, thou knowest, O God, I am thine."

And it was with that inner faith that he met his end. When he was led from the concentration camp at Flossenburg to the gallows where he would be hanged, just days before the fall of Nazi Germany, he knelt in his prison uniform and prayed. William James had little interest in organized religion or in religious doctrine as such. But he understood religious experience. I think that here was a life experience that would have impressed him and, perhaps, made him wonder just a bit about the faith that undergirded that experience.

Chapter Nine

RELATING TO OTHER RELIGIONS

For over twenty years, both as a *Monitor* journalist and an investment banker, I never made a trip to London without stopping in for a visit with an elderly Christian Science teacher there. We had been introduced fortuitously by my own teacher, and she apparently found it worthwhile to spend some time with me—perhaps just to get my views on what was happening in America. She usually had her housekeeper get together a noon luncheon and would invite other friends in for a conversation. Our last visit would have occurred in 1988, just after a short business trip on which my wife accompanied me. We phoned her early on the day we were to see her and got a series of busy signals. Finally, I concluded either that her phone was out of order or that something had happened to her. Later that day, one of her closest friends called to say that she had passed on during the night and been found by her housekeeper early the next morning. She must have been past ninety years of age, but she was one of those vibrant, almost ageless people who kept my own study of Christian Science alive at the time.

I always found her views on Christian Science practice challenging, no more so than when one day she said to me, "Just because you're a Christian Scientist, don't think you know all the truth." I pondered just what she meant by that and did not think to challenge her any further on the point at the time—a lost opportunity. But now I think I know what she meant, and this chapter will eventually bring that out. I also found, through knowing her, that even the most experienced Christian Scientists do not always agree on every point of their religion—also a fact that I will refer to later in this chapter. My own teacher and mentor, for instance, had had a most strict standard about resorting to medical help, even when a healing did not seem to come about. I respected that, and still do, but she had a somewhat different mindset. "It's better to still be here than not, isn't it?" she said, in effect, to that point. And when her phone would ring, her stock question of a patient would usually be, "Are you all right?" She was never afraid to ask the humanly compassionate question, even though she was also ready to supply an answer from what she would have called a higher level.

The personal remembrance above may seem a most indirect way to lead into the subject of this chapter, but I think you will see my reason as we go on. This chapter deals with the ways in which Christianity in a wider sense and Christian Science in a narrower sense relate to other religions and thought systems today. It is not a subject that would have come up for very many Americans one hundred years ago. When *The Christian Century* magazine was renamed in 1900, it was widely assumed by the Western Christian world that Christianity was on the way to becoming the predominant world religion. Yet today it is quite clear that Christianity is but one of several worldwide religions. While Christianity has spread in recent years in sub-Saharan Africa and in South Korea, so has Islam spread in the Western world. And Buddhism has found a permanent home in America. In Los Angeles alone there are over three hundred Buddhist temples, and not all of them represent the same groupings of Buddhists.

To the degree that one is actively practicing his or her religion, he or she will be noticed. In this highly secularized society, one who stands for something religious actually stands out. So it is important to know how one can best convey to others what he believes in, or adheres to in his deepest moments, when he is asked. And the obverse side of this is that one cannot tell others if he does not have a clue to what their own belief-systems mean to them.

A century ago, a knowledge of non-Christian religions was essentially nonexistent among the public. Even knowledge of Jewish practice and rituals was virtually nonexistent, although there were Jews in American cities of any size. One measure of what was known, particularly of Eastern religions, is evident in the very few statements Mary Baker Eddy made, at least in her published writings, about Eastern religions.

In *Science and Health,* her only reference is a negative one: "The eastern empires and nations owe their false government to the misconceptions of Deity there prevalent." This is no more than the probably common view of China, in particular, at the time of the Boxer Rebellion.

A year later, when the original Mother Church edifice was dedicated, some of the newspaper accounts of Christian Science connected its growth to the increasing interest in Oriental religions. Religious writers were also not well versed in other religions, so it is not strange that they made connections where none existed. A writer in the Chicago *Daily Inter-Ocean,* for instance, wrote of the "wave of idealism" sweeping the country "under the guise of Christian Science, and ingenuously calling on a closer inquiry into Oriental philosophy...." And the writer for the Kansas City *Journal* said that the "belief and service" of the church satisfied a mystical taste that had "shown an uncommon development in this country during the last decade, and which is largely Oriental in its choice." Mrs. Eddy had always emphasized that the revelation, or enlightenment, that had come to her had come solely through the Bible and her own Christian upbringing. So it is easy to see why she was alert to stopping any budding confusion about its source.

At about the same time (1893), she did have a rudimentary acquaintance with what was beginning to be talked about in the religious world. In one of her private letters to a student, she had written: "In answer to Rev. Mr. Easton's questions relative to the Hindus will say, the true sense they entertain of humanity is the best part of Buddhism. And the sense of taking no thought for what we shall eat or drink, is Christ-like, for Jesus taught it. This therefore is far from self-mesmerism, rather is it a native Christianity which presages science—a denial of personal life and sensation that admits the existence of Being where it is, namely, in God not man, in Spirit not matter, in Soul not sense." (Courtesy of the Mary Baker Collection, L04690)

In commenting on this in my biography of Mrs. Eddy, *Persistent Pilgrim*, I noted that her references to Buddhism were not entirely correct, but they do show some knowledge of the general tone of Buddhism as well as her appreciation for the commonality that might inhere in any of the world's great religions.

When the Columbian Exposition was held in Chicago in 1893, one of its most significant events was the convening of a World Parliament of Religions. Christian Science was represented at the Parliament, and many Christian Scientists regarded this recognition as a triumph of their new religion. However, Mrs. Eddy saw the Parliament as giving new exposure to Eastern religions, and while she was not opposed to any religion, she was fearful that Christian Science might be confused in the public mind with Hinduism or Buddhism. So her attitude toward its inclusion at the Parliament remained at best equivocal.

This recounting of her attitude at the time is not only for the possible interest of someone who is a Christian Scientist. It also illustrates one of the possible pitfalls of religious dialogue—a confusion over systems that may appear to have more similarities than they actually possess.

There was a time when Christians felt that their mission was to convert the world. That remains the mission among many evangelicals, and they comprise the largest bloc of missionaries still active outside the United States. Some experts in the field estimate that as many as ninety percent of the missionaries fall into that category. However, given the pluralistic religious world that is now so evident, many feel that the best way forward is to *live* Christianity rather than promote it.

Harry Hoehler, a Unitarian-Universalist minister for fifty years, has written a lengthy monograph entitled *Christian Responses to the World's Faiths*. Almost every page of what he has written emphasizes the need for the greatest humility in approaching this subject. The language we use to describe *the* human-divine encounter, he says, is "inevitably limited, the product of events and thought patterns of a particular historical and cultural tradition. As such, it is bound to delimit our understanding of God and God's relationship to us. People of faith, Christians included, are faced with the incompleteness of their knowledge, humbly struggling to understand, with the limited and imperfect language tools they possess, the meaning of God's manifestation for their lives."

When asked about Jesus' admonition to his disciples to go into all the world and preach the Gospel, Karen Armstrong responded, to a group at Chautauqua, New York, that to her this meant only that the Christian message was available for anyone who would receive it. No longer was salvation offered only to the Jews. The world of Jesus' time knew only Judaism and non-theistic religions.

Hoehler has a chapter in which he discusses and disagrees with the idea of a world religion, a combination of the "best elements" in the present religions. He finds this an unrealistic proposition for several reasons. For one, those who think that a single religion might emerge out of a pluralistic religious dialogue generally describe it as a codified version of their own religion. For Christians, it is some version of Christianity. He quotes a Hindu thinker who sees it as a kind of Hinduism, in which the other faiths may survive as lesser exemplars of what Hinduism is to him.

A more important reason for the unlikelihood of such a development is the fact that not all of the major faiths agree on what their goals are. He quotes one person who says to those who say we are all striving for the same mountain top, "Let's wait until we get there to see if it's the same mountain." For traditional Christians, the goal is... For Hindus and Buddhists, the aim is to achieve a personal union with the Absolute, which they do not call God, but in some ways at least conforms to what the Judeo-Christian tradition would call God.

In the nineteenth century, James Freeman Clarke wrote a book entitled *Ten Great Religions*, in which he foresaw Christianity as the one most likely to become the world's religion. He found every one of the other religions lacking some quality he perceived in Christianity. About Brahmanism, for instance, he wrote, "[it] is an eminently spiritual religion, but it is deficient on the human side." Yet, notes Hoehler, "A difficulty with such chauvinistic apologetic is that, more often than not, it is unfamiliar with the range and depth of the ethical dimension of so broad and layered a tradition as Hinduism. This very tradition, let us remember, with its emphasis on non-injury, active good will, tolerance, and antimaterialism provided the intellectual and spiritual framework for Mahatma Gandhi, one of the great transformers of human conscience in modern times." And Hoehler also notes that, while Gandhi knew and appreciated Jesus' Sermon on the Mount, he did not think he needed its addition to make his own faith more complete.

Many Christian theologians are quick to see evidences of Christianity in other faiths. There surely is, since mankind is on a common spiritual quest. But the way in which Christians sometimes talk about areas of commonality is actually patronizing to the adherents of the other religions. It is ignorant of, or ignores the fact, says Hoehler, " that [others] do not see their [own] deepest loyalties as defective glimpses of Christian truth. As a consequence, it rejects the possibility that other faiths might have genuine worth of their own, independent of the claims of the Christian Gospel."

He quotes E. L. Allen, who has written on comparative religions, to the effect that the same God Christians worship may have spoken in different ways to other peoples and cultures within the context of their own experience. "Since divine truth in its fullness is beyond the grasp of any one person or group, committed Christians can testify only to that portion of God's truth which grasps them. They can never claim to know God's truth whole...they must always be open to the possibility, if not the likelihood, that their neighbor of another faith possesses understanding of the wisdom and love of God *which they do not have* [italics added]." This, I think, is what the British Christian Science teacher meant when she admonished me that I did not know all the truth!

The fact that we may learn from other religions does not mean, of course, that they have everything in common or that they either start from the same set of assumed beliefs or share the same ultimate goals. Hoehler says, "Orthodox Christians and Muslims believe in a personal God. Vedantin Hindus by and large do not. Most Christians and Hindus believe in divine incarnations, Jews and Muslims do not.

Hindus and Buddhists believe in reincarnation, the Semitic religions do not."

Even among Christians who believe in the importance of the life of Christ Jesus there is disagreement. "A good many orthodox Christians...would balk at the notion that sinful human beings can seek and find metaphysical harmony and unity with God. In the first place, God finds them. Beyond that, they seldom lay claim to an absorption type experience of at-one-ness with God which such harmony often presupposes. They may experience God's claim upon them and God's call for obedience; but they remain forever finite, created, identical neither in substance nor experience with the Holy One." I quote Hoehler at length because the passage shows clearly what many Christian Scientists may find in an initial discussion with other Christians—that there needs first to be some agreement on how one identifies the word "man."

If people of religion may never agree on any single religion, what does bind them together? Their common humanity binds them together, whether they are humanists, theists, or Buddhist nontheists. But among those who share some personal interest in their religion, there certainly is a sharing of the belief that one's religion is an important part of his or her life. This resonates with Jung's and James's statements in my first chapter about the importance of religion in one's life, that it adds a vitality that enhances every other part of life. Hoehler quotes Joachim Wach, who wrote *Types of Religious Experiences,* to the effect that "religious experience is the most intense experience of which a man is capable."

shared is the knowledge that each person to whom religion is an important facet of his life is embarked on a similar journey. Stanley Samartha, a former Director of the World Council of Churches' program to dialogue with other religions, wrote that "the essential feature of all religious life is its pilgrim nature," that we are all on the way, so to speak. And Diana Eck, a professor of comparative religions at Harvard, has written in similar fashion, "In dialogue we speak with people who, like ourselves, are on the way....As pilgrims we seek a destination we know only in part. But we share not only our destination on the 'other shore;' we share, most significantly, our journey."

If we can learn anything from others on that journey, or if through our own living we can perhaps give something valuable to our fellow journeyers, how can we best do it? Obviously, dialogue is the answer. But dialogue is more than a mutual sharing of the elements of a belief system or, in terms that would mean something to a Christian Scientist, the details of the metaphysics of Christian Science.

Wilfred Cantwell Smith, who was Director of Harvard's Center for the Study of World Religions, said once that we cannot package religions "as if they were discrete units readily open to coherent systematization." He continues, "The concept of essences simply cannot accommodate the inebriating variety of humanity's religious life." A religion, besides its doctrinal core or the metaphysical statement it makes, includes the kind of worship that is involved. It includes the daily practices, such as prayer or reading or meditation that its individual adherents take part in. It may include certain rituals. It may include acceptance of elements of authority over the individual's life, such as is the case with Roman Catholicism. We cannot share the essence of our religion with another if we are not able to communicate these other elements as well. Furthermore, most religions undergo some change over time in at least some of their practices.

Finally, even within religions, not everyone agrees on everything. In Christian Science, for instance, what became part of the religious tradition very quickly may or may not be of importance to everyone who tries to practice Christian Science. Smith believed that "since every cumulative tradition exhibits a wide range of internal diversity, people located within a tradition find themselves constantly confronted with other people who stand somewhere else within the spectrum of that same cumulative tradition. In other words, reconception can occur when Christian faces Christian as well as when Christian faces Hindu."

Moreover, one religion does not dialogue with another religion. It is one *individual* of a certain religion who dialogues with another *individual.* It is two persons each somewhere within the spectrum of their respective religions who meet and talk. And their dialogue can be the most meaningful if it somehow involves an understanding of all the elements making up a religious tradition, not just its official teaching.

In dialogue, one must be prepared to learn something as well as to hope he has helped the other person to a better understanding. Through understanding something of another person's religious allegiances and practices, he may see better what some part of his own religion means to him. Hoehler concludes his book with the statement that Christians who believe that God's love has been shown in many ways throughout history also "believe that no one's understanding of God's truth is absolute in this life; they support dialogue as providing a window through which a greater measure of truth might come to light."

And he mentions an interesting fact about Vatican II, the theological discussions that took place in Rome from 1962 to 1965 under Pope John XXIII. Until that time, the Roman Church had referred to non-Christians as pagans and unbelievers. When asked about the reasons for the elimination of this kind of terminology in the Church, the Pope's private secretary explained that it was the result of an awakening the future Pope had had when he was Apostolic Delegate in Turkey. After "observing Muslims in their prayers, speaking with Muslims about Allah, he could no more speak of pagans, of unbelievers, but only brethren in the one God the Father." Again, it was through personal, individual encounter that something had been learned.

This discussion might not have seemed very important a century ago. But today we are living in a society that is pluralistic in more than a racial or nation-of-origin sense. We are pluralistic in a religious sense also, and if we do not understand what this implies for each one of us, it could be as dangerous and costly to our progress as a society as the old racial stereotypes and misunderstandings were for so long.

I will end this chapter with a story from Diana Eck's recent book, *A New Religious America*. In it, she details the extent to which non-Western religions have grown in recent years in America. One of the most poignant stories in it concerned two religious groups in Fremont, California. In 1993 the United Methodist church there and the local Islamic Society broke ground for two new edifices—a church for the Methodists, a mosque and school for the Muslims.

Fremont, in San Francisco's East Bay, is a mixed community and a good staging ground for an experiment in "getting to know you." The two groups built next to each other on a frontage road they named Peace Terrace. The ultimate aim is for their geographic proximity to lead to their getting to appreciate each other's religious views with greater understanding. They did their landscaping with each other's needs in mind, and they have shared some of their facilities and parking. When I was a child, we knew of no mosques in Chicago, and I doubt that any Christian church would have broken ground jointly with a Jewish synagogue. So we have come a long way in two generations.

If learning about each other helps us to share what we have in common and to appreciate what may be helpful in what we do not have in common, what about learning from each other when the others' views are supposedly our own? That is, are our own churches a true community for sharing, and do we even need such a community? That is the subject of the next chapter.

Chapter Ten

CHURCH AS COMMUNITY

In the previous chapter I leaned heavily on the booklet written by Harry Hoehler, who had done such a thorough job in looking at the ways in which we may—and should—profit from each other's faith traditions. In this chapter I must make a more serious admission: I not only have leaned heavily on a book by a Catholic monk in Toronto, I have also learned much from it and have been forced to look at my sense of community in my own church.

Ronald Rolheiser lives in an order of Oblate monks in Canada. He wrote a book from the heart, entitled *The Holy Longing: The Search for a Christian Spirituality*. Rolheiser thinks there are four elements in spiritual growth: private prayer and morality; the search for justice; "mellowness" of spirit, which I would take to be a general sense of love, kindness, and gentleness; and, finally, community. In my own life, I would have automatically linked the first three requirements. Perhaps because Protestantism is less organized and generally less hierarchical, and Christian Science in particular is so individual in the prayer and practice it encourages, I think, in my own experience, the sense of community has seemed less important. After reading Rolheiser's book, that no longer seems to me to be the case.

Describing spirituality in mere words is perhaps a fruitless exercise. He gives some of the definitions that must partially satisfy him. Of those he mentions in his book, the one that resonated with me was this from Saint John of the Cross: "...the attempt by an individual or a group to meet and undergo the presence of God, others, and the cosmic world in such a way so as to come into a community of life and celebration with them." If we are to try to find some common bonds with people of other faiths, what about tightening the bonds we have with those with whom we share the same faith? Sometimes it is easier said than done, just as it may seem easier to be kinder to the gardener on some days than to our spouse.

Rolheiser is not naïve as to the difficulty one sometimes finds in loving the people in one's own church. He says, "A parish-type family is a hand of cards that is randomly dealt to us; and precisely to the extent that it is truly inclusive, will include persons of every temperament, ideology, virtue, and fault. Also, church involvement, when understood properly, does not leave us the option to walk away whenever something happens that we do not like. It is a covenant commitment, like a marriage, and binds us for better and for worse."

Examples from early Christianity may not seem appropriate today, but the New Testament certainly gives a picture of people meeting often in small groups to worship together and to support each other. There were even some elements of the sharing of resources at first. Rolheiser notes, "Part of the very essence of Christianity is to be together in a concrete community, with all the real human faults that are there and the tensions that this will bring us." And in a most convincing sentence, he writes, "...anyone who says that he or she loves an invisible God in heaven and is unwilling to deal with a visible neighbor on earth is a liar since no one can love a God who cannot be seen if he or she cannot love a neighbor who can be seen." A part of the way we can tell how we relate to God, he says, can be measured by how we relate to each other.

Moreover, much of the healing the world needs can come about only through joint action. Not only the action, but the prayer that leads to action can be more effective if it is jointly supported. Speaking about the church as the body of Christ, as Paul also does in I Corinthians, Rolheiser says that if its members are the body of Christ, then God's presence in the world today depends on those members. When we pray for justice or peace, we bear some responsibility for the answer to that prayer, he says. We do not expect a remote God to act, but as the living body of Christ, our religion demands of us that we become involved in bringing about the result we have prayed for. I think that this is a stand that all Christians must feel some resonance with, even those who do not take the "body of Christ" allusion quite as literally.

Of course it is relatively easy to attend church and be part of a congregation if one thinks he is "getting" some good out of it. The converse to this is that we should also go to church to give, but we often do not consider what it is that we can bring into church with us.

Gary Gunderson, who is Director of Operations of the Interfaith Health Program at the Carter Center, has written a book, *Deeply Woven Roots*, that discusses the need for church as part of the community structure. Because the search for what people in general label "spirituality" and its connection with health has become so popular, he sees a need to place both spirituality and health in a broader setting than merely individual well-being.

He writes about a forest of redwood trees. "The most important things to understand about a redwood tree—and about a community—is how it passes life on," he writes. "Where does the next generation come from? Redwood trees don't usually spring from individual seeds; they spring from the roots of older trees. I was lying in the middle of what had once been an ancient giant of a redwood tree. The trees surrounding that circle were, in fact, the young ones. They reached 250 feet into the air, but they were the children."

Starting with how trees grow in a redwood forest, not from seeds but from the roots of mature trees, he sees a spiritual community in much the same way. He says that ever since he saw this as a metaphor, "I have thought of a congregation and its surrounding community as a forest, an image that leads us into the future in two ways. First, we can see ourselves as one of the trees, taking comfort in the complex richness of our enduring connections. Second, we can see ourselves as foresters, with the humble patience of stewards who measure their contribution in terms of decades, nurturing and defending a living process."

Surely anyone who has ever survived teaching what seemed at the time a recalcitrant Sunday School class can find some comfort in thinking of himself as one of those foresters preparing for the future. If we are tempted to think that we do not find enough of a sense of community in church and can just as well grow spiritually by staying at home reading and praying, we might consider whether even our slightest participation in church as community may help someone else.

Echoing the thoughts of Rolheiser, Gunderson sees the interaction of a faith community as essential to building the strongest kind of faith: "Much is written today about the role of spirituality on a private level, nurtured apart from the inconvenience of community....But while one would expect faith to be valuable at the personal level, that is not primarily where it is formed. For the most part, we learn of faith through others, hopefully by what we experience in our families, but often as adults, from others whom we trust or admire because of what we see happening in their lives. Faith can be nurtured in solitude, but it is rarely born in isolation."

Chapter Eleven

THE CHRISTIAN SCIENCE CHURCH

I've told you what Christian Science has meant in my life. I think it can mean the same in yours, but that is for you to find out individually. However, before bringing this to a conclusion in some kind of coda that I have not figured out yet, there is one more thing to talk about—the Christian Science church. Even as you work out your own religious inclinations, or more important, your religious commitments, your religion and your church are not identical with each other.

Church

When Mrs. Eddy began teaching the rudiments of Christian Science healing, she had no intention of starting her own church. She saw her system of spiritual healing as reinstating something that had been lost over the centuries, but certainly not as replacing any of the essential Christianity of the churches. But her early students found that their experiences as healers were not welcome news in at least the churches of Lynn, Massachusetts, in the 1870s, and they wanted to have a church experience like everyone else did in those days. So it was only in 1879 that she established the first Christian Science church. Then, after some unhappy experiences with her students, some of whom thought they could run the fledgling church better than she could, she dissolved it in 1889. Then she went up to New Hampshire in semi-retirement, and in the peace she found there over the next few years, she realized that some church organization was necessary to protect what she had begun. It still is, but many factors have crept in that did not have to be considered a century ago, and that is what this section tries to deal with—always from my own experience. And I realize that there are many Christian Scientists who would not agree with me, although I expect that most open-minded Scientists would find some part of what follows to be something that resonates with them.

The Manual

This small book contains the rules governing the operations of The Mother Church, the headquarters organization in Boston. It was written over a period of several years to deal with the problems of the growing church, as well as to set out the basic form of organization: a Board of five persons, self-perpetuating, with no term limits. This has been criticized at times as a mistake, since a small group such as this is not apt to appoint people unlike its present membership. (However, I have never seen how an elected board—elected by whom, the entire membership?—would be an improvement. The Harvard Corporation is also a perpetual group of five with a similar charter.) Over the years, it was general knowledge that the Board would not take any major action without unanimity. If this was indeed true, it prevented the Board from making hasty decisions, but probably also resulted in a Board that was too slow to move with the times. There is some discrepancy in the Manual language as to whether any of its rules could ever be changed. A charter with no chance of change could in time grow archaic. For instance, Christian Science class instruction, the two-week course that is the basis for entering the public practice of Christian Science, is not supposed to cost more than $100, the current price of a good dinner for two in an upscale restaurant. There is ample evidence that the Directors of the Church are aware of some of the problems the Manual causes them. In recent years, the format of Christian Science lectures has been greatly altered: sometimes they are called workshops, for instance. While lectures are still given, they are not the bread-and-butter means of imparting current information to most people. Yet, while efforts have been made to conform the lectures to current needs, many members of the Church have objected even to that as a violation of the Manual. One of the general counsels of The Mother Church in the late 1980s asked one of the Directors if he thought they had the authority under the Manual to make changes in it. Yes, replied the Director, but out of respect for Mrs. Eddy, he did not think they ever would.

The Directors

The Directors are men and women who come from a background of successful Christian Science practice, and they have also become Christian Science teachers. This presumably gives them the background they need to watch that the teaching and practice of Christian Science remain sound, that is, in keeping with the metaphysical system. But it does not guarantee their performance in running a major business operation. In the past twenty years, the Church has run its endowment dangerously and unnecessarily low. In the mid-1980s, it embarked on a well-thought-out plan to bring its news-gathering arm, *The Christian Science Monitor*, into the mainstream of today's media by reaching into radio and television. The TV operation proved to be costlier than at first estimated, and it was difficult to bring in non-church partners, particularly when many Church members spoke and wrote so vehemently against this expansion of the *Monitor*, which they regarded as being destined to remain solely a print product. The Treasurer of the Church warned several times that funds were running low, but felt that he had no ultimate authority in the matter. There were no Board members at the time who had any substantial financial experience, and it seems remarkable that they could have overruled their own Treasurer, who did. Again, after funds were built up in the 1990s through a shrinkage of the organization's overhead and good financial market performance, the Church embarked on a new plan—to build a library to house archival documents that otherwise would have gone out of copyright in 2002. By the time this project (also criticized by much of the membership) was completed, the Church's treasury was also severely depleted.

The Church's government should not be judged solely on its financial management, of course. But in today's competitive, commercial environment, financial management is certainly a key element of an organization's management. Moreover, a 501(c)(3) organization is dependent to a good extent on the goodwill of those who contribute to it, so the opinions of the members cannot be entirely ignored, or at least not ignored for long. Back in the early part of the 1900s, when the Church was just getting organized to build the large Extension to The Mother Church, Mrs. Eddy wrote to the Board that it would be a good idea to get a good businessman on the Board.

Even though the Board reconstitutes itself as I indicated, there often does not seem to be the learning from experience that there should be. Over the past thirty years, there must have been at least five or six major reorganizations of the *Monitor*. But how much was learned from the past reorganization? Much of the same ground is gone over time and again: What is the ultimate market? Who is the competition? What is the role of advertising in such a unique paper?

As much as most Christian Scientists want their Church to succeed as an organization, the question they must ask themselves is, Is this the kind of management to which I want to commit my funds? So far the Church has benefited from the gratitude of Christian Scientists for what their religion means to them. But will that be enough in the future?

Teachers and Practitioners

Among the duties of the Board—perhaps first among their responsibilities—is to maintain the quality of those who practice and teach Christian Science. Without correct teaching, the metaphysics of Christian Science could be confused with a myriad of other mental systems. Often confused, as in the case of William James, with "mind-cure" systems in general, it is essential to maintain its connection with the entire Christian message of compassion, concern for others, purity in one's own living, and in an unselfish motivation in all of one's activities. If these elements are missing in the teaching, there is something essential missing. In Mrs. Eddy's own time, she was most concerned with the teaching, and when she published *Miscellaneous Writings* in 1897, she asked that there be no teaching of classes that year. She thought that a careful reading of her own selected works, which is what that compendium is, would do more for one's understanding than teaching.

Today there is a general belief among Scientists that the teaching is uneven at best. How the Directors could be expected to monitor the teaching of over one hundred authorized teachers is difficult to say. Where medical issues are concerned, as they increasingly are in an era of advanced medical technology and a longer living population in general, it becomes even more difficult. More frequent meetings of the entire body of teachers might help work through some of the current ethical issues involved. But such meetings would need to involve an honest discussion among all the participants. More frequently, the groups that the Church has assembled on various occasions have been less than frank in their discussions with each other. This can be the case especially where a teacher's "license" to teach is held, in effect, by the Directors.

The monitoring of the practice of some one thousand or more Christian Science practitioners would be even more difficult. A practitioner's relationship with his or her patient is a confidential one, and what one person says to another can always be misinterpreted or even used with a dishonest motive. The medical and psychiatric professions have groups that do hear complaints against their own practitioners, but the anecdotal evidence is that no professional group likes to take action against its own members unless there is overwhelming evidence of abuse.

In the case of Christian Science, one of the causes for which complaints have been lodged against both practitioners and teachers in the past has been through the alleged "mixing" of spiritual prayer with medical aid. The lines that may be crossed here are many, and again, because of the widespread prevalence of medical advertising and undoubted success in many areas not previously reached by medical means, there are fewer and fewer clear-cut answers. What this amounts to, in my opinion at least, is that it is so difficult to monitor the teaching and particularly the practice of Christian Science that the individual is left to his own prayerful guidance in seeking help from anyone. This is not a criticism of the Church, but a simple statement of fact that seeking help from others must always be an informed, individual decision.

Community and Your Church

When it comes down to you and me going to church, it is our own local church that matters most of the time more than any organization at the top. In most of Protestant Christianity, churchgoers are almost solely concerned with their own church and its minister. By contrast, Christian Scientists have no minister, or pastor, other than the Bible and the Christian Science textbook, as is explained at the start of every Sunday Sermon. When the Church was growing rapidly, Mrs. Eddy could not find enough ministers to take care of growing congregations. She also found among some of the ministers who had converted to Christian Science less than a full understanding of the radical nature of her metaphysical system—that is, speaking in absolute terms, the allness of God and his spiritual universe and the resulting nothingness of matter and evil. So she determined to have the Sunday Sermon be the same Lesson that Scientists read throughout the preceding week. The Lesson is highly metaphysical, and while it includes lengthy stories from the Bible as well as individual Bible verses to make certain points, it may strike the stranger as too impersonal. After fifty years of listening to the Lesson, I have to agree. (During much of this time I was a Sunday School teacher, so I have not had a continuous half century of sitting in church!)

In today's world of a fast media culture, this kind of service seems almost lifeless to me. Now, there may be some churches that have ministers whose preaching is just as lifeless. Emerson remarked once that the minister he heard talking gave no inkling that he had ever lived or loved or grieved—that the world outside seemed more real than what he was hearing from the pulpit. So Mrs. Eddy was not alone in seeing the pitfalls of a poor minister. If someone were to ask me how I would organize a Christian Science church today, I'm not really sure. This is why it may not matter if the branch churches gradually dissolve and their congregations move to the more open Protestant churches where they will be welcome. Would they take Christian Science with them? I have known of one person who worked all week in a major position at The Mother Church in Boston, but decided to attend the local Unitarian Universalist church on Sunday as well as attend spirituality meetings the minister held during the week. Many people knew she was a Christian Scientist and welcomed insights she shared from her own study. Is not this perhaps what Mrs. Eddy hoped would happen back in 1870?

Having said that about our Sunday service, the Wednesday evening meeting is another matter. Here the First Reader reads short selections from the Bible and *Science and Health*, usually for not more than fifteen minutes. Then members of the congregation share remarks that include not only their healings in Christian Science, but also the entire gamut of experiences they have had that they relate to their practice of Science. Coming in the middle of a busy week, these meetings can provide many people with guidance and inspiration for the rest of the work week. Even here, changing times have taken their toll. Fewer people come out at night, either because they are too tired from the day's work or do not want to be out in their cars after dark. And a weekly commitment may seem too much for many individuals. Here again, changing situations will cause whatever goes on within the Christian Science church to become more flexible.

One thing that is missing from a Christian Science service is a choir. I suppose that anyone who has ever had to manage an amateur choir may say, "Good riddance." But I remember my teenage years in Oak Park, going to the First Presbyterian Church most of the time, where we had both a very good amateur choir and a paid quartet, some of whom were singers in the Chicago Opera. Moreover, some of the finest music in the Western musical tradition is church music, and even when some of the interpretations that lie behind the music may not agree with every tenet of Christian Science, the beauty and inspiration of the music remains for anyone to draw on. But choirs take churches of some size, and in general, it may be just as well that Mrs. Eddy did not provide for choirs. In the future, though, I think there will be a few very large churches and many small, maybe even informal ones, and I hope the large churches have a choir. As a teenager, I sang several times with our Oak Park High School a cappella choir in the Rockefeller Chapel at the University of

Chicago. I enjoyed it! And even today one of the highlights of our Christmas season is to hear the Harvard and Radcliffe choirs do their Christmas service at the Harvard Memorial Church.

To get back to ministers: One of the advantages of having a live minister who speaks from his heart each week is that it allows the church to consider its teaching and mission in the light of current events. I sometimes feel that the metaphysical emphasis in our Lessons overlooks the ethical demands of Christianity. It isn't always enough for the average person to just hear the story of the Prodigal Son read again, or to hear the parable of the Good Samaritan. What does this mean in light of the suffering in the Sudan? What does our laying waste to the environment have to do with the stewardship we are entrusted with? A church can go too far in preaching only on the events of the day, but there should be both a connect to the world we are living in and a call to the courage that Christians should have (as in the extreme case of Dietrich Bonhoeffer) to make one leave a church service not only lightened in heart and more hopeful, but also determined to make a difference.

There is also reason to conclude that a church is better served by having a full-time minister than depending solely on volunteer boards and committees. This varies depending on the demographics of every area, of course. But with the American habit of moving frequently, with both spouses now working most of the time, the continuing existence of a church, including the important matter of taking care of its physical structure, for instance, demands major committee work by its members if they are to carry on without a full-time minister. Of course, to have a minister means there has to be a congregation large enough to support his salary. Most Christian Science churches today could not do that. But how large should a church be to really function in today's society? Mrs. Eddy stated in her *Manual* that there had to be sixteen members! Surely she did not have in mind a church with a major budget to meet. Such a church could meet in most people's living rooms, where the members could read the Lesson Sermon together and perhaps have a short discussion to share their insights.

If we are to have local churches, the minister can provide more than a sense of continuity. He or she can help to provide the basis for the sense of community that I have just discussed and that every person needs—whether he knows it or not. This requires that a church genuinely wants to be open, to provide that sense of community. Until recent years, Christian Science churches would not allow anyone to join who used tobacco or alcohol in any form. The Mother Church led the way in abolishing this requirement over a decade ago, but it has still not been generally accepted by many. This requirement was put into place in the early 1930s, and one close friend estimated that the main reason membership in the church entered a decline was this one change. He may have exaggerated. However, in every church of which I have been a member, there have been spouses who could not join (usually the male) because of this requirement.

The statement I have just made needs some softening. Requirements for membership were instituted because it was felt that Christian Science, *being* science and not just religion, had to be practiced according to rules. Someone who was a lush or a sensualist could not be assumed to be serious about practicing Christian Science. However, someone who bordered on being an alcoholic or who was living a life beyond the bounds of what was considered upright behavior would have been unlikely to want to join himself with a group of Christian Scientists. The rule about alcohol was particularly annoying to many, since in virtually every Western country some form of alcohol was and remains an important part of the culture—and sometimes even of the daily diet.

What we all need is to see church as an institution that brings us together, that helps us to share our common humanity and hopefully to encourage us to express more of our Christ-nature as the children of God. It is the only community place where we can share our deepest needs and get our lives more in order. It is not like the workplace—we do not gather because of common work goals. It is not a political party, where we share a common social or economic agenda. It is not a social institution, where we practice some kind of one-upmanship. It, ideally, is the place where we meet in complete equality as God's children to learn more of our true identity and how to bring what we know to bear on our lives and the lives of our community. Anything less is not church today. When we ask whether we can do more for ourselves, or for our community, or even to advance Christian Science, we need to have this in mind. Where should your church be? That is a question you can answer only for yourselves. I cannot answer it for you.

Chapter Twelve

FINDING YOUR OWN WAY

When I started writing this, I mentioned that a high-school teacher had once gently reminded me that what we think or know about God makes a big difference. You can see that what religious people have thought about God has had a good deal of variety to it and that concepts have not been static for the past two thousand years. Yet today, because "God" can mean so many different things to people, all the way from the theistic personal God of the Old Testament to an immanent presence that many would say is only a subjective feeling, the word is sometimes avoided.

Ronald Rolheiser, whose book *The Holy Longing* I discussed in Chapter Ten, writes, for instance, that "even within our churches, it is easier to have faith in Christianity, in a code of ethics, in Jesus' moral teaching, in God's call for justice, and in the human value of gathering as a community, than it is to have a personal faith in a living God." Maybe that is why so many Christians emphasize Jesus in their preaching, since they agree that in him they find the most perfect example of God at work.

Yet what God means to each of us individually is the starting point from which we hope to draw our values, the strength of our convictions to act, our entire sense of purpose in life. So, with that as our starting point, how do we hold on to whatever conviction we already have and even strengthen it?

Prayer and Meditation

For starters, one must take the time. Everything we hope to excel at takes time. The body does not last without sufficient nutrition. Our health is affected long term if we do not get enough physical exercise, and so on. The condition of our thinking is not as obvious, but it also needs its nutrition. You may recall Shakespeare's phrase "As a man thinketh, so is he." The only prayer that is offered in the Christian Science church service is the Lord's Prayer, which Mrs. Eddy felt covered all human needs. But when Scientists pray in church, they also have a period of silent prayer, in which they can listen to what God is telling them. Praying is not primarily to inform God of anything. In fact, in the terms in which I described what God means to me today, God is not someone somewhere listening to me. I only need to listen to him, or to confirm in my own thought what I believe God, as the infinite Mind, knows about me, as his reflection or idea.

Meditation may take the form of dwelling on some religious ideas or writings that need to be absorbed more deeply. It can consist of silent listening, something most of us find the hardest thing to do. Protestants in general are less used to this than are Catholics or Buddhists, who more generally hold special retreats for this purpose. Dietrich Bonhoeffer introduced the practice of daily prayers and meditation in the seminary he briefly ran, but he tried to inculcate this practice as a habitual one even during the war years. "The daily, silent meditation upon the Word of God," he wrote, "with which I am concerned—even if it is only for a few minutes—must be for me the crystallization of everything that brings order into life, both inwardly and outwardly. In these days when our old rules of life have had to be discarded, and there is great danger of finding our inner order endangered by the rush of events, meditation gives our life a kind of stability."

To quote Rolheiser again, he notes, "Among classical spiritual writers, there is this leitmotif: In order to sustain yourself in faith you must regularly (most would say daily) spend an extended period of time in private prayer. Failure to do so, they warn, results in a certain dissipation of the soul, even when our sincerity remains intact." For Christian Scientists, of course, there is the weekly Lesson Sermon from the Bible and *Science and Health*. That takes most of us close to thirty minutes to read thoughtfully. However, even that can become a kind of rote exercise unless it is combined with some more time given to praying over specific problems that need to be solved or in simply trying to listen for God's guidance.

But praying does not take place only in the quiet closet of individual consciousness. It can take place on the street or in the subway. Henri Nouwen, the Dutch Catholic writer, says of prayer, "[It] means to think and live in the presence of God. All our actions must have their origin in prayer. Praying is not an isolated activity; it takes place in the midst of all things and affairs that keep us active."

Keeping the Sabbath

I have also told you how dull Sundays seemed to me as a child almost seventy years ago. Wow—has that changed! Sunday has become almost like any other day. In some ways, that is progress, I guess. It is certainly more convenient to be able to go to the grocery store when you are out of milk or orange juice. But the day has become a major sports day for big-league sports, and the entire weekend is seen by many as two days of entertainment and "catching up" for another hard week ahead.

I was struck by how much I have gone along with this gradual erosion of what Sunday once meant when I heard David Weissbard give his talk about the Ten Commandments at Chautauqua. Weissbard is not a theist; he is a humanist Unitarian clergyman. His talk on the Commandments was his own "take" on what they should mean for our behavior today. When he came to Sunday, he was downright old-fashioned. It is a day for worshipping that which deserves to be worshipped and remembering that our ordinary activities of the week, essential as they are, do not constitute our whole life. He told how, as a Boy Scout, he loved to do the map-reading exercises, where the Scouts had to follow a set of compass directions in order to arrive at a prescribed point. Periodically they were supposed to stop and get their bearings, to be sure they were on the right course. The Sabbath should occupy the same position in our lives, he felt. It is a time to remind ourselves of the ultimate goals of life and reassure ourselves that we are on the right course.

Abraham Heschel notes in *God in Search of Man* that all of the words in the Ten Commandments are simple ones: They can all be easily translated into other languages. Yet one word has not been translated—the Sabbath. "Remember the Sabbath day...." Writing glowingly of the Sabbath, he says, "The Sabbath is an assurance that the spirit is greater than the universe, that beyond the good is the holy. The universe was created in six days, but the climax of creation was the seventh day. Things that come into being in the six days are good, but the seventh day is holy. The Sabbath is *holiness in time*. What is the Sabbath? The presence of eternity, a moment of majesty, the radiance of joy."

With such language, one feels challenged to ask himself what the Sabbath ought to mean today. For the Christian, who celebrates this day on Sunday, the knowledge is added that their chosen day of Sunday is also meant to commemorate the risen Christ. Our Sunday habits are not going to return to the 1930s. But in addition to daily prayer and meditation, there is reason to consider what this day could mean to our civilization if it consisted not just of habitual churchgoing (for those who still go to church), but also some thought as to what the original institution of this day was meant to signify.

Progress

I told you about the Christian Science teacher who reminded me that I did not have all the truth! This reminded me of a passage in Hermann Hesse's *The Glass Bead Game*, the novel for which he won the Nobel Prize in 1946. In it, Josef Knecht (the German word for servant) is a seminarian in an institution that maintains the value system of Western culture. I would describe it as a kind of secular Vatican. Knecht is on the way up to some position of importance in the organization, but he continues to have his doubts about its purpose. At the climax of the novel, he becomes the Grand Master of the institution, only to defect for what he thinks is a greater freedom to progress as an individual outside the confines of the organization. But in the instance I was reminded of, he asks the man who at the time was the Grand Master about the nature of truth. The extended conversation goes like this: "The whole of world history can be explained as development and progress and can also be seen as nothing but decadence and meaninglessness. Isn't there any truth? Is there no real and valid doctrine?" The Grand Master answers: "There is truth, my boy. But the doctrine you desire, absolute, perfect dogma, that alone provides wisdom, does not exist. Nor should you long for a perfect doctrine, my friend. Rather, you should long for the perfection of yourself. The deity is within you, not in ideas and books. Truth is lived, not taught."

This is why God is not "learned." He must be experienced to be real for you. When we say that we know something about God, of course we do not know it in the same way we know some specific fact. But we mean that we believe it in the sense that Anselm talked about in the eleventh century—we act upon it with conviction. This is not passive belief, but knowing in a religious sense. Paul wrote, "For now we see through a glass darkly; but then face to face: now I know in part; but then shall I know even as also I am known."

I have quoted at length from writers of different religious traditions—from Roman Catholics, from Jews, and from Protestants. Virtually everything I have been saying here could have had some quote from the writings of Mary Baker Eddy, which have buttressed my own religious convictions for over fifty years. I hope they might do the same for you as you go along in life. But by bringing myself up to date on what other religious thinkers have been doing, I thought it remarkable that we were arriving at much the same point. That is important for Christian Scientists to know, since within the boundaries of one's own religious reading one can forget that others are making a similar, even if not identical, religious passage.

For anyone who is not a Christian Scientist who may read this, I would hope that he would find confirmation of these thoughts in the writings of Mrs. Eddy. After more than fifty years of almost daily reading of the Bible and *Science and Health*, I remain amazed at the brilliance, for want of a more complete word, of that book and the way it encourages, coaxes, and leads human thought. When Lyman Powell, an Episcopal clergyman who wrote one of the early biographies of Mary Baker Eddy (in 1930), was discussing his work with leaders of the Christian Science church, he told them in effect that he thought Christian Science was something larger than could be contained within the confines of that church organization. (Maybe a bit like Joseph Knecht in this case?) What I think he was driving at was that whatever truth there was here must be shared in every way possible with other religions, with other individuals looking for spiritual guidance, and that it might not always come merely as a result of the church's own activities. As a minister himself, he was also aware of the links that Christian Science has to past theological developments, and he saw Christian Science as definitely within the mainstream of Christianity. I hope, in the time I have given to discussing some of the past history of Christianity, that this has become clearer.

Most significantly, the spiritual journey is a lifelong quest. It has immediate demands and immediate rewards in a fuller life. But we are never there—we are continually looking for more light, and we hope to know more of the ultimate reality tomorrow than we do today.

To return a final time to William James: He wrote that the religious life in the broadest terms possible "consists of the belief that there is an unseen order, and that our supreme good lies in harmoniously adjusting ourselves thereto." He also wrote, "It makes a great difference to a man whether one set of ideas, or another, be the centre of his energy; and it makes a great difference...whether they become central or remain peripheral to him." But for the individual who makes a serious turn to what we would call God, there is the promise, or reward, that "fear and egotism fall away; and in the equanimity that follows, one finds in the hours, as they succeed each other, a series of purely benignant opportunities. It is as if all doors were opened, and all paths freshly smoothed."

PART TWO

Autobiography

Although I began my conscious life on a sunny Sunday afternoon, October 13, 1929, even a brief record of it for the sake of my children's and grandchildren's possible future interest must begin with the background of my parents and their parents. Our family, all of northern European extraction, were relative latecomers to the United States.

Of the Nennemans, I know next to nothing, except that my grandfather came over as a young man, probably in the late 1870s, and that he and a brother owned a grocery store on the west side of Chicago. I have an old tintype that shows them standing in front of their store by barrels of who knows what. Whether he lost the store because of his reputed alcoholism, which cost him his life in 1914, or had a falling out with the brother (a more modern-day question that might arise) I do not know. Or perhaps he had the store right up until the time of his death. My father told me that his father had come from Pomerania, also that he thought they had some connection with Stettin. Stettin, a port on the Baltic Sea, is today part of Poland, and Pomerania is split between the reunited Germany and Poland. I have never followed through as I should still do, as there are some sixteen Nennemans listed in the Berlin phone book. Since Germans until this generation did not tend to go far from their birthplace, I assume that at least some of these Nennemans came from Pomerania and that some relationship is waiting to be confirmed. (Nennemann originally had two "n"s on the end, a typical German name ending. I do not know when the second "n" was officially removed. The grocery store sign carried only one "n." On the other hand, my father's confirmation certificate from about 1910 showed the old German spelling.)

My grandfather, Wilhelm Nennemann, married Charlotte Nagel. Charlotte was born in 1861. Charlotte was the first child born to Conrad Nagel and Dorothea Lamp, who were married on January 22, 1860, by a Pastor Link. Nagel was a teacher in the Lutheran church school in a village known at the time as Pleasant Ridge, Illinois. A Reverend Wagner was pastor of the church at the time Charlotte was born. This information is in my Aunt Millie's handwriting on the back of a small picture painted by her father, showing the church and the small house in which Charlotte was born. Charlotte was the only one of my four grandparents to be born in the United States.

Charlotte and Wilhelm must have been married about 1880, as their first child, Walter, was born in 1881. Arthur followed in 1883, and Rose in 1887. Then, after another four-year interval, three more children followed: Ray in 1891, Julia in 1893, and my father, William, on December 2, 1897. Of their childhood years I know very little, except that Ray, Jul, and my father, being the three youngest, obviously were close together in their childhood pursuits. Rose was ten years old when Dad was born, and they had a special closeness all their lives because he said she looked after him so much when he was a young boy. Rose, Ray, and Jul also were extremely close, partly because Rose (whom we all called Doe) had no children of her own and was very solicitous of my two cousins, Shirley and Paula, who lost their father when they were small children. Some of the closeness of my father's brothers and sisters, as well as their great affection for their mother, can be sensed from Ray's letters written during the First World War. Their entire childhood was spent on the west side of Chicago. Although they were probably not well off, even in the terms of 1900, they all loved music, and both my father and Ray talked of the many operas they had seen as they grew up and of being supers at times in large opera scenes.

My mother was one of three children born to Bessie and Gustav Edward Peterson (Gustav Elof Petterson), who both emigrated from Sweden during the great emigration of the 1880s from Smaland and Skonig (over one-fifth of Sweden's population left southern Sweden). Bessie was born in 1860 as Bengta. Her name was apparently changed by an immigration officer's fiat to Swartz when she entered America. How she adopted the name Bessie from Bengta I do not know. One of my cousins, Gordon Peterson, thinks that her parents were hoping for a boy and says that Bengt was a masculine Swedish forename. Disappointed in what came forth, they may have simply added the "a." My uncle, Paul Peterson, who was a missionary, visited their hometowns in Sweden, and it is from his records that I know their respective birthplaces. Bessie and Edward, as my grandfather was called, were apparently acquainted in Sweden, as one of the stories I remember their telling is that when the second to arrive came through immigration, the first met the other with the terse and unemotional greeting, "Well, you're here." Edward was ten years junior to Bessie. He was born in 1870 and lived almost until his 105th birthday in 1975.

Bessie learned and spoke English quite well. Edward, on the other hand, always had a much more pronounced accent and did not write the language well. I do not know the exact dates of their peregrinations. I believe that early on they went to Chicago. But Edward was attracted by the chance to get cheap land in Alabama and moved the family there with little knowledge of the climate or culture of the Deep South. Paul was born in 1895, my mother, Fannie Madelyn, in 1896, and Marguerite in 1898. At least Paul and my mother were alive during the years of the Alabama episode, as I have heard her speak of it. Alabama did not work out, and they then moved to a small farming community, Tennessee Ridge, near Nashville, Tennessee. My mother spoke of her childhood largely in terms of what she remembered of Tennessee Ridge, and we visited it once, in 1941, just before the

Second World War. From Tennessee Ridge, they eventually moved back to Illinois, where my grandfather practiced carpentry in Rockford, a city in northwestern Illinois with many Swedish immigrants. From there they moved to Chicago, where he became the gardener and groundskeeper for a wealthy family, the Otises, who lived on the lakefront south of Jackson Park in Chicago. My mother's teen years were spent mostly in Chicago. When my grandfather had a heart attack after recovering from the Spanish influenza at the end of the World War and could no longer do strenuous physical labor, Mrs. Otis got him a job as an elevator operator in the Otis Building on LaSalle Street. This would have been in 1918 or 1919, and he kept going up and down in this elevator until he retired at the age of seventy-five in 1945.

The Nennemans were German Lutherans. My uncle Walter was the first to break with the rigidity of the Lutheran Church, and he and his wife, Millie, joined the Presbyterian Church. Following the First World War, both Ray and Jul became interested in Christian Science, which had phenomenal growth in the Chicago area. They both became lifelong Scientists, although neither ever joined the Church. Ray once said in effect that he was glad to be out of the Lutheran church and felt no need to be in another. My father had some interest in Christian Science and on occasion went to lectures with them. But (according to my mother) my grandmother was saddened by the defection of so many of her children from their religious upbringing, and until he married, my father continued to accompany his mother to church, whatever his inner development may have been. After his marriage to my mother, they began a lifelong accommodation to each other's religious views, which was, in my opinion, never satisfactorily resolved.

Whether my mother's parents were brought up in the official Swedish church, which was Lutheran, I do not know.

Their subsequent religious experience makes it more likely that their country upbringing had Pietist aspects to it. There had been a "free church" movement in Sweden since the early nineteenth century, although any church other than the state church was not officially recognized. In Chicago my mother's religious experience was in a specifically Swedish Baptist church, but at some point before she was married, my grandparents had become affiliated with the Pentecostalists (this makes the Pietist background seem plausible). My grandmother was about to be operated on for the removal of gallstones. After prayers were said for her in her church, the gallstones either passed or were dissolved overnight, and no operation was needed. In any case, whether they were Baptists or Pentecostalists, they were at home in the evangelical tradition.

My parents met working on LaSalle Street, the banking street of Chicago. My mother, I believe, did not have formal schooling beyond grade school. She had lost some time in that period during which she was recovering from rheumatic fever. In any case, she had secretarial school training and was as well equipped as any high-school graduate for the secretarial work she did. My father apparently did not finish high-school before going to work; in his papers I found high-school equivalency graduation papers for work he had to complete before enrolling in the Chicago Kent College of Law in 1923. They were both working in a bank at the time America entered the First World War. I do not know if they knew each other then or not, but their serious relationship must have started around 1920. They became engaged in 1923. Long engagements were common in those days, and they did not marry until 1926; but at least one reason for this was that my father wanted to finish law school, which he was doing at night, before marrying.

My mother went on a three-week vacation to California in August and September of 1920. It must have been somewhat unusual for a mere secretary to take so much time off in those days. She recorded her impressions of the trip in a lengthy journal, the only written record she left other than one year's diary, which I kept (after discarding all the rest of her diaries after her death in 1980). What I did read of her later diaries had little in them to show her real feelings: The diaries seemed to me to be more a record of what happened each day. But the 1920 journal tells a lot about her as well as the state of society at the time, and I have kept it. She was fairly light-hearted, compared to the mother I knew as a child and in her later years. She wrote doggerel verse on the trip and seemed to enjoy seeing the homes of movie stars in Hollywood, and in general there was nothing in the journal to indicate the kind of judgmental attitude she took toward the world later on. One night she hid under the bed of her two traveling companions, both young women, with the intent of teasing or surprising them. (She was twenty-three years old at the time.) I never read this journal until after her death, although it was included in a photo album and was nothing that she had hidden (but there were multiple old photo albums in the family).

Sometime around 1922 her brother, Paul, left his business in Chicago, convinced that "the Lord" had called him to be a missionary in eastern Europe. In recent years it has occurred to me that this religious event, which so altered the course of his life, may have impressed my mother with the need to think more seriously herself. I do not know. But there was also a strong ascetic streak in the kind of church-going she engaged in. Card playing was out; movies were out; dancing was out. When my father told her he had bought tickets to see Puccini's *Madama Butterfly*, she went with him only under duress. As a child, I remember her telling me that she cried throughout the opera (and I do not think it was because of the tragedy unfolding on stage). She felt that, if she had not gone with my father, he would have broken off their engagement.

At any rate, the long engagement was followed by marriage on September 25, 1926, at my Peterson grandparents' house on the south side of Chicago. Mother did not want to live west, possibly because she did not want to be so far from her parents. My father was still working in the Loop (downtown), and they agreed to get an apartment on the far south side of the city in a location close to the Rock Island suburban train line. The two addresses I remember my mother telling me about were 9101 Loomis and 9132 Laflin, both very close to each other. My mother had a stillborn male child in February 1928. He was born at seven months, and labor was brought on by some near accident in their car that happened on snow or ice. My mother was a very sentimental person, and she often referred to this event. In any case, she became pregnant again within a year, and I was born on Sunday afternoon, October 13, 1929.

Until this time, with the exception of the stillborn baby, their marriage had been proceeding smoothly. My father was the only one of his family to have a professional degree, and although he said he had never intended to practice law full time, he thought it would enhance his career in banking. Less than two weeks after my birth, the stock market experienced the infamous Black Thursday, October 24. From this moment on, my parents' fortunes turned. My father was in the market and apparently heavily margined. In addition, he had by this time joined a bank in the stockyards area on the south side called the Peoples National Bank and had become a stockholder in it. Under Illinois law at that time, bank shareholders suffered double jeopardy—that is, they could lose not only their whole equity, but also be liable for an amount of debt equal to the face value of that equity. But disaster did not strike all at once. The stock market rallied somewhat, and the most stupendous declines still lay ahead in 1930. Moreover, the bank he had joined was well run and would probably not have closed had it been entirely independent. However, under the laws or practices then prevailing in Illinois, it was common for smaller banks to have a tie-in (possibly some indirect ownership) with a major Loop bank. In this case, the Loop bank went under sometime in 1932, and that event triggered the collapse of the Peoples National Bank.

My father never talked to me in detail about these years. In one sense, the remainder of his life was a slow but very cautious comeback from the personal trauma of the Great Depression. Most of what I have related here came via my mother.

Close to the time of these events, they decided to expand their living arrangements and moved to a new bungalow even farther south, at 10517 South Campbell Avenue. I need to describe this neighborhood, as it became my home for the next nine years, and its peculiar environment undoubtedly had something to do with shaping me.

The area around Chicago is notoriously flat and uninteresting to anyone who has ever seen a hill, let alone a mountain. But fifteen-thousand years ago, when the last glaciers receded, they left a lake bed where Lake Michigan is that was somewhat larger than the present-day lake. In this lake was a narrow spit of land a mile or so wide and six miles long. The lore I grew up with was that this was inhabited by the Indians. When the lake finally receded to its present boundaries, this island was left as a higher piece of land on the flat prairies of Illinois. It was called "blue island" by the Indians. As the city of Chicago grew, two parts of this island became suburban-type developments, Beverly Hills and Morgan Park. To their south there is a separately incorporated town actually called Blue Island. The homes in Beverly Hills were built mainly in the 1920s; the location was good for executives working in the stock yards or in the steel mills ten miles east along the shores of Lake Michigan.

Running the north-south length of this area is a street called Western Avenue (perhaps it is also the longest single street in Chicago, as it stretches north to the Evanston line). West of Western Avenue was not as developed; in fact, about half a mile west the remains of the island dipped down to the plain, and as a child I often rode my bike out to the sand dunes that remained as evidence that a lake shore had once been there. Campbell Avenue was two blocks west of Western, and the 105-106 block had been filled with neat bungalow-type houses just before 1929. My parents lived there for a year, and my only memory of that house is our leaving once for a trip to Indiana. However, just behind the bungalow was a block of empty lots, with the exception of 10508 Artesian Avenue, on which was built, just before the crash, what was to have been the first of a row of three-story brick apartments. Artesian Avenue was just one block from Western, and perhaps the development plan, although that is too grandiose a word for whatever planning went on in those days, was that the street next to Western should be reserved for apartments, as a buffer to the private houses farther away from Western Avenue.

I am not certain whether the collapse of my father's bank was the reason for moving, or simply that the owners of the bungalow wanted it back. My parents lived in the bungalow for only one year, from 1932 to 1933, and in the fall of 1933 we moved to the apartment that was to be my sense of home until I was almost in the eighth grade. By this time my father was unemployed, but each day he would walk the block to the streetcar and journey into the city to look for work. Of course, there was virtually nothing new happening in these years. We had a 1929 Oldsmobile that he kept in the garage, and I can remember the day he was finally able to sell it. It had not been used for some time; I believe he could not afford to have the necessary repairs done on it.

So, from the time I was four years old until I was twelve, I lived as an only child on a street where we had no neighbors. On one occasion, when another family in our apartment had a boy slightly older than I, my mother did not approve of my playing with him. Moreover, when I started kindergarten in the fall of 1934, she got permission for me to attend Clissold School at 110th Street and Western. This was not in our school district, but she or my father apparently thought that this was a safer place for me to go—it did have one less through street to cross. Exactly what her reasons were I do not know, but it meant that whatever children there were in the surrounding neighborhood all knew each other from school, while I was regarded as if I were some kid who went to private school.

From sometime in 1932 until sometime in 1934 my father was unemployed. Besides being a banker, he had passed the Illinois bar and may have tried to get some legal practice. But this had not been his career intention, and I doubt that it brought in any income in the midst of the Great Depression. He did have business cards printed—WTN, Attorney at Law, 5000 Ashland Avenue. I remember them mainly because of the address and that we used up a lot of printed stationery over the years. I think one of his business friends let him use the office space. His oldest brother, Walter, was well established with R. R. Donnelley & Sons, and my mother says that he gave us some money at first. Then, in September 1933, he had a heart attack at the age of fifty-two and died. One of my earliest memories, in fact, of the apartment we lived in is of my cousin Eunice calling on the phone in tears and asking for my father. I was apparently already answering the phone, because I called to my father, who was out working in the garden he had planted. He collapsed in grief. I remember sitting with him in our living room while he seemed absolutely disconsolate. I could not understand what had happened, of course, but I had never seen either parent in this state. Eventually he gathered himself together, and the three of us made the long trip by streetcar, L (the elevated) to the Loop, and another L up to the North Shore, where they lived in a gray stone apartment house in Ravenswood.

The garden in which my father had been working is one of the central characters of this period in my life. The typical lot sizes in this part of Chicago were 40 by 125 feet. My father had taken the two lots next to our apartment and developed a vegetable and flower garden. It had intricate grass paths and a central lawn surrounded by variously shaped flower beds. Later, when he was again working, this became his main hobby and so continued for the rest of his life. But in these first years, my mother later said it also gave us a lot of our food for part of the year. They raised wonderful corn and beans; we always had abundant lettuce and tomatoes for salads during the summer. We also ate a lot of spaghetti and canned brown beans during these years. Each year the flower garden became more complex, and the perennials always needed splitting. So there was an opportunity to share the plants with friends, and many a summer evening, people he worked with would come by in their cars and take away cut flowers or whole plants that he gave them. When he could afford it, he began to buy a few shrubs from a local nurseryman: just beyond this part of Chicago there were still truck gardens that grew produce for local consumption. He became well acquainted with the owner of one of these. In later years he helped him acquire more property (as his lawyer) and later to sell it also. There are a few pictures of the garden, but unfortunately home photography had not entered the color phase before World War II, and the pictures give only a dim idea of what he had created out of prairie land. Of course those two lots comprised only a quarter of an acre, but they seemed far larger in my mind then—and still do today.

My school must have been an anachronism in the Chicago system: We had good teachers. After I got over crying at being left there (for kindergarten), I think I adjusted fairly rapidly. Remember, I had had no playmates other than my cousins until I was five years old. My memory of learning to read is that I was slow at first to catch on. But once I was past that hurdle, I was generally competitive with my class. In the second grade, the brightest of us, or the quickest learners, were separated from the rest and put a half-grade ahead. So all of my class were probably somewhat quicker than the rest of our cohort. Later on, in fourth grade or so, we were seated according to our grades, and I was always in the first seat in the first row. This may not make for popularity with one's classmates, but actually there was a group of boys and girls that I felt very close to. Although we could not play together after school because of my living too far from all the others in that school district, we did make after-school dates—probably by the fourth grade—and when I could ride a bike later, I would spend much time after school with two particular friends, Jack Kottemann and Teddy Naylor.

Once in fourth grade I had to make a coal mine as a special project, and my parents patiently gathered coal dust in the basement of our apartment and helped me make the three-dimensional project. It subsequently won some kind of award. I was also Father Marquette in a school play about the exploration of Illinois by Marquette and Joliet, and I enjoyed being costumed as the priest and learning to baptize the Indians in Latin. I imagine these events would have been considered fairly innovative in a big-city school in the 1930s, and my subsequent schooling certainly showed that Clissold had been as good a place to start as any suburban grade school might have been.

The lack of after-school playmates undoubtedly contributed to my doing more things on my own. As early as my sixth birthday, my father began teaching me how to play the piano. Sometime after he was working regularly again, my parents got me a piano teacher. She would come to the house to give lessons, and I remember being impressed that she had an automobile, while my parents were still without one. I also sat under the dining-room table for long periods looking up at the table, so being alone did not apparently make me overly ambitious at that stage of my life. As for playmates, though, my cousins were the main supply. I had two cousins living in Oak Park, Shirley and Paula, whom I saw less regularly. But my mother's sister, Marguerite Engholm, had two children, Roger and Carol, who were just a year older and a year younger respectively. Paul, their father, worked for Bethlehem Steel, so they lived on the far south side of the city. They came regularly to visit, at least once a week, and my mother and I frequently went over to their house as well. I remember them chiefly in terms of playing hide-and-seek as well as games of Monopoly® when we were all a bit older. My Uncle Paul also contributed a modest sum toward our upkeep during the years my father was unemployed. Since he did not have a large income, this was extremely generous of him and something he and my aunt never mentioned to me in later years. When my mother died, I gave them something more than she had left them in her will; these were extremely modest sums as well, because by 1980 my mother was almost out of funds, but I hope they understood the gesture.

I had five other cousins, but they entered my life only on occasion. Eunice, Walter's daughter, was half a generation older. She married in 1938 and moved to Evansville, Indiana. She married Calvin Brazelton, and they had one son, Bruce, who at last count lived in a suburb of Columbus, Ohio. My mother's oldest sibling, Paul, had four children, Paul, Gordon, Doris, and Robert. They lived on the north side, and particularly when we had no car in the 1930s, it took an hour or more to reach their house by various streetcars. We were together chiefly on some birthdays and always on Christmas Eve, when the Scandinavians tend to have their exchange of Christmas gifts.

Shirley and Paula's father died in 1936, and Ray, who had never married but had kept house for his mother until her death in 1930, rented a large house in Oak Park, where he became a sort of foster father. My Aunt Julia and the two girls lived on the third floor in rather crowded rooms, while Ray and my other Nenneman uncle, Arthur, had their bedrooms and bath on the second floor. Arthur was the black sheep of the family, and according to my mother, Ray had taken him in to his own apartment when his mother died, in accordance with her last wishes. Arthur had liked to drink too much in his early years and had lost one good job. He worked for the U.S. Postal Service and either played or talked about the horses whenever I saw him. Besides his bedroom, Ray also had a sitting room on the second floor, where he played his opera records and burned incense. He was the only person I have ever known who burned incense. This may have been a throwback to a habit that was popular in the 1920s. In any case, his sitting room always had a delicious smell to it. I always thought that Ray was a very generous person because of what he had done for his sister. That part of the family had a somewhat suspect reputation as far as my mother was concerned, because Ray and Julia had become Christian Scientists after the First World War. But they always seemed lively and happy whenever we visited, and it was only much later that I learned of the inevitable tensions that must arise when a brother and sister live together under such circumstances. Ray could act the father figure when he wanted and disappear from the scene when that pleased him. He regularly drove the twenty miles to our apartment in Beverly Hills on Sunday mornings, when Jul and her girls were at church, to have a visit with my father and to linger in the garden. From their conversations I first gleaned something of the tensions that might exist, although it did not matter much to me at that time. He, Jul, and my father were close to each other their entire lives, and I think it was only Ray and Jul's understanding and counsel that kept my father going during the last fifteen years of his life. In 1936 Ray bought himself an aquamarine Oldsmobile, one of the gaudiest colors yet on the road, and I would sometimes wait in the living room on a Sunday morning for his shiny car to come around the corner.

We could take no trips during the Depression, but after my father started working again he sent my mother and me to be with Marguerite, Paul, Roger, and Carol in a Swedish summer colony on the Michigan side of the lake for two weeks. This was an area that boasted very high sand dunes, comparable to what one still sees in Truro on Cape Cod. I loved these weeks as well as seeing my father come to fetch us at the end of them. And Mother felt at home with the Swedish friends of her youth. There were numerous afternoon coffee parties as well as the gossip that flows freely in a small community of like-minded people. Since most Swedes had married Swedes, I can appreciate now how difficult it must have been for my mother to have adjusted to my father's family. It was not that they were particularly Germanic, only that they were not Swedish.

In 1939 I had my first trip beyond Lake Michigan. My aunt Rose, or Doe, invited us to come to Louisville for a week. I am sure we could have gone at any time, but this was the first time my father felt he could afford even a small trip. We still had no car, and my Uncle Paul met us early in the morning and drove us to the Greyhound stop on the far south side, where we took a Greyhound bus to Louisville. It was magic! It was a warm March week, and we visited Lincoln's birthplace and My Old Kentucky Home, among other places. I wrote a letter to my grade-school friends telling them about the marvels of Kentucky. Doe had no children, and all her life she was extremely generous to Shirley, Paula, and me. (When she died in 1972, she left me a fourth of her estate, the portion that would have gone to my father had he been alive.) But her generosity in these years was what I remember most—the Christmas boxes with eight or ten presents for me. Many of them did not cost much, but they were all things she had picked out thoughtfully. And whenever she traveled, she would send us postcards from the places she visited.

Then, at Christmas 1939, my father bought a second-hand car, a 1935 black Ford sedan. We were again as mobile as other American families. One small incident that revealed something about Ray: We spent Christmas Day, as we always did, with Ray and Julia in Oak Park. My father was proud of his acquisition and took Ray out for a ride. Ray had just bought himself a new 1939 Oldsmobile, and he had probably had a drink or two before we arrived (no one ever served alcohol in the family, probably because of Art's problem; neither my father nor Julia drank alcohol). Anyhow, Ray, in some way I cannot remember, made fun of the new purchase, and this revealed a side about him that made me uncomfortable. Nevertheless, after that, we had two summer vacations before World War II curtailed the family driving. In 1940 we went to Louisville and then south to the Great Smoky Mountains and to Asheville, North Carolina. My parents had spent their honeymoon there and wanted to see the city once again. Then, in 1941, this time with a 1940 Chevrolet that saw us through the war years, we more or less repeated the trip, but also stopped at Camp Tullahoma, where a friend of my parents from their church had been called to active duty. They took pictures of me on a tank, etc., and I, least of all, was aware that a war was almost upon us that would change our outlook for the rest of our lives. (I was almost twelve that summer.) That was also the trip on which we found Tennessee Ridge, one of the farming communities Mother had spent some time in as a young girl.

Besides my neighborhood, school, family, and the constricted economic times in which I grew up, there was church. When my parents married and moved to the neighborhood they were living in when I was born, they found a community church—St. Paul's Union Church—that seemed to be a good compromise between their different religious backgrounds. Composed of people from the various mainline Protestant denominations, it customarily had a Presbyterian minister. The church had many people in it who came out of an evangelical tradition, so as the years went by my mother found like-minded people. It also had a men's Bible class, in which I suspect there was a much freer spirit of inquiry. My father often said he got more from the Bible class, which met at the same time that the women were teaching Sunday School, as he did from the minister's sermons. There was never any thought that we would do anything else on Sunday morning besides go to church. The church was not social in the sense of the members getting together socially. By its nature, it attracted people from up and down the ridge that was Beverly Hills. But the various friends my parents had there probably provided the social glue they needed during the 1930s.

So, when I turned twelve, it was natural that they (Mother, especially) should think about my joining the church. We had just moved to Oak Park in September 1941, but they continued to attend St. Paul's. It seems unnatural now that I should have joined a church in a community in which we no longer lived, but I must have expressed some interest. My father had been an elder of the church for at least six or seven years, and I am sure he was looked on as one of its pillars. It did seem like our church home. For my mother, the only drawback was that the church did not practice total immersion the way the Baptists do it, and she felt that anything less was not a complete baptism. I had not been baptized at birth as the Lutherans do it, because she did not believe in infant baptism. Anyhow, the morning of my joining the church, December 7, I met with the consistory (the elders) of the church for the requisite interview. Each one said something kind to me (I knew them all well), and when it came to my father, he started to say something and then completely broke up. I was at a loss to understand what had happened, and he went on through his tears to say how much we had seen God see us through and what our religion meant to us. He was not accustomed to talking a lot about God, and I sensed just a little in his emotion the hard times he had lived through virtually since my birth, but about which he had never talked to me.

This would have been enough emotion for one day. But on the way back to Oak Park, he suggested that we stop at the restaurant at Chicago's Midway Airport (then the main Chicago airport) for lunch. While we were having our lunch, reports came over the radio about bombs dropping on Pearl Harbor. All the way back to Oak Park we listened to more early reports of the bombing, and by the time we got home, the event of the morning—my joining the church—was virtually forgotten. In a few hours our whole world had changed. For my generation, whatever experiences we had during the Great Depression, plus coming to maturity during World War II, would remain the core of our background and affect the way we looked at events for the rest of our lives.

* * * *

That part of my early life, growing up on the far south side of Chicago, seemed to flow as a single unit as I recounted it. But before proceeding to my years in Oak Park, which were also a formative period of my life in other aspects, there are a few specific episodes I remember from the 1930s that have come to mind often enough that I think I should recount them here. They are unconnected, but I am relating them here, as far as I can remember, in roughly their chronological order.

1934 or 1935, probably when my father was still unemployed: Late one afternoon Mother gave me twenty-five cents to go and buy a dozen eggs at the egg and milk store on Western Avenue. This store was in the middle of the 105-106 block, and our apartment was closer to 105th Street. She told me explicitly not to cut across the grassy fields separating Western and Artesian, but to walk on the sidewalk going around the block on three sides. I cut across the field, though, and stumbled and dropped the quarter. She came out and, as I remember, searched with me in vain for at least one hour to find that quarter. We did not find it. I do not believe I was punished (although my father did spank me on several occasions), and eventually she found another quarter and went with me to buy the eggs. I used to tell our children this story, because even in the 1960s a quarter still represented some kind of money. Today I can only say that the episode stuck with me as an example of how hard up we must have been.

1937: My father was again working and had the use of a bank car at night. The Outer Drive bridge was opened, and we drove downtown to go across it the first night, for which we got some kind of sticker. This was the night that FDR gave his Quarantine Speech, the first warning of what was coming from Hitler's Germany.

1937: My father was about to take me to see Walt Disney's *Snow White and the Seven Dwarfs*. This was the first time I learned by experience how much my mother thought the theater, including movies, the work of the devil. A long argument ensued, my mother ended up crying, my father called off the trip and went out to the garage to play with his gardening things, and I found him there later almost in tears himself. He tried to excuse my mother and said she was a good Christian, but that he could not understand her unreasonableness about some things.

1938 or so: I used to play alone quite a bit, and one image that remains with me is going along the street in my red wagon and occasionally seeing an airplane overheard going southeast. This was in the early days of regular commercial flights; Midway Airport was in a square mile between 55th Street and 63rd Street and a few miles west of us. I assume that all the planes going east went around the south end of Lake Michigan in those days, so this would have been a regular flight path for a good percentage of the flights at that time. I wondered if someday I might fly in an airplane myself.

Labor Day, 1939: Ray picked us up and we went somewhere toward Joliet for a family picnic. Hitler had invaded Poland three days before, I believe. Anyhow, I will always remember Ray's saying, "Well, it looks like here we go again, Will."

As I read over what I have written thus far, it seems to me that I may have overemphasized our relative poverty in the 1930s. Compared to what the prospects must have looked like for my parents before 1929, that is true. I was aware that my father had financial problems, mainly from what my mother would tell me. I was also aware that my father had been unemployed, then employed for a couple of years by the Federal Receivership, then out of work briefly in 1938 before he went to work for the National Bank of Commerce, where he remained until their merger in 1963. I think we were often a month behind with the rent. My parents stoked the furnace boiler for the three apartment units for at least two years, for which they got a slight reduction in their rent. On the other hand, I also remember my mother's often giving food to tramps, who came to the door. In those days, unemployed men made marks on the concrete sidewalks to give signals to others as to where they might get a handout.

There was one other thing that balanced all this: In 1929 my parents were probably better off than any of their brothers or sisters, with the possible exception of my uncle Walter, who was half a generation older. They had good furniture and, in particular, set a fine table with good linens, some of which we still have seventy years later, good china, sterling silver flatware and some other pieces of silver, as well as a lot of gold china that was popular in the 1920s. At the major family reunions at Thanksgiving and Christmas, I do not remember any sense of lack. In fact, my memory of a good table has probably combined with Kathie's memory of a more luxurious childhood and more elegant cooking than I was used to, with the result that we have always placed a high value on the table, from wanting to give elegant dinner parties to how we ate together daily as a family and used the dinner hour as an essential part of family togetherness. But on to Oak Park.

* * * *

Since the spring of 1938, my father had been working in a post-Depression bank, begun in 1936, at Madison and Crawford on the west side of Chicago. This was actually very close to the neighborhoods he had lived in as a child. Until the end of 1939, he had no car and spent probably an hour each way on two streetcars getting to work and back. But it was also almost an hour's drive, and he needed to be closer to work. My mother did not like leaving the south side, where her parents and her sister lived, but at the same time it was becoming too difficult for my grandparents to keep house themselves. So they agreed to come and live with us, and my parents found a rental house in Oak Park, just four miles from the bank and also where Ray, Jul, and my cousins Shirley and Paula lived. In October 1941 we moved to 514 Clinton Avenue, Oak Park, and this was home for me until my second year in graduate school at Harvard. The house was a cream stucco building, built about 1910, on a 37½ foot lot. My father's gardening days were not over, but his gardening activities certainly became constricted. My grandparents had one of the three bedrooms. I had a small bedroom with an unheated sleeping porch off of it, so that in parts of the year I could still have an overnight guest. The living room had a heated sun porch in front of it, almost as large as the living room itself. In the evening, my grandparents tended to sit in there, and we would use the living room. But they always went to bed very early, and until 1945 my grandfather was still getting up at 5:30 in the morning to go to work.

By that time I was in the second half of seventh grade. I had a bicycle, which overcame the problems of living on an empty block, and I had two very good friends, Jack Kottemann and Ted Naylor. Yet I do not remember being particularly sad about moving, and my parents knew that the Oak Park schools were among the best in Illinois. My introduction to the school, though, left me with the impression that they thought I was a nincompoop, having wasted seven grades in a Chicago school. I remember conversations about my possibly having to be set back half a grade. Then, when my eyes were tested and they found I needed glasses for nearsightedness, they told me that I would undoubtedly do a lot better in school once I had glasses. Anyway, all these first impressions on their part were soon undone, and I was at the head of the class again—something not to be envied in a newcomer. I was only at Emerson School a year and a half, but during that time, on December 8, I remember our being called to a classroom where we could hear President Roosevelt declare a state of war. I remember our teacher telling us she hoped this would be the last time this would ever occur. In eighth grade, I was elected President of the Junior Civic League. This was my first and only experience in school politics, and I am still amazed that I ran for the job, since I was still mainly an outsider in the school. I think I won only because I ran against three females and their vote was split.

Most of what I remember about Oak Park are the four high-school years. Although we continued to live there most of the time I was at Harvard, my "real" life after 1947 was in Cambridge. And how can I summarize those four years, maybe the most formative years of anyone's life? I made new friends, experienced the first surges of sex, had some intellectual challenges, and began to question the roots of my religious upbringing. It is impossible to put all of that in perspective, which only serves as an individual example that history as personal memory is not highly reliable.

High school, first of all, was big. Emerson School had been roughly the same size as Clissold. But OP High kids came from eleven such grammar schools in Oak Park and a few more in River Forest. Altogether there were thirty-two hundred kids, about eight hundred in a class. That made Harvard easier four years later, but in 1943 it seemed formidable. In February 1943, when I started high school, the United States was just beginning to win World War II. The fact that we were engaged in our country's biggest war was there in the background, but I do not remember it being something we thought or talked about daily. The Chicago Tribune did run great four-color war maps, and I did follow the war, but I think that was as much from talking with my father and Ray as from anything at school.

Music became an important and integral part of my life during high school. While we were still living in Chicago, my parents had paid for me to have piano lessons, and I had developed a good sight-reading capability. After I had adjusted to my new grade school, though, they got me a teacher, Ruth Wilkins, who probably had more professional credentials than the first one. In any case, I studied with her all through high school and even during the summers when I came home from Harvard. In high school I was in the *a cappella* choir and was also one of its pianists when we were not singing *a cappella*. My sight-reading ability ended up being useful when I was the practice pianist during rehearsals for Gilbert and Sullivan operettas (the orchestra was brought in, only with great difficulty toward the end of rehearsal). I am not an artist, and I have never gone as far as I probably should have with piano. But I still enjoy it, still am learning new pieces, and I think that music was one of the things that made my high-school experience much more pleasant. It was perhaps my alternative to sports, in which I considered myself a dunce and never had much interest.

Through my working with the operettas, and also because I took a summer school public-speaking course with him in 1945, I became acquainted with Cookie. Knowles Cooke had come to teach at OP in 1944 from Ottawa Hills, a suburb of Toledo. He was a product of the University of Chicago, a bachelor, and one of the first intellectual "challengers" in my experience. He was a close friend until he died in 2000 at the age of ninety-three. I also became one of the editors of the high-school literary magazine, *Tabula*, and the two faculty advisers for that enterprise, Max Hohn and Rececca Burt, became important figures in my life. In Miss Burt's case, that influence was to last for several decades, as she was a Christian Scientist and one of the people who first made me think seriously about my religious presuppositions.

Because of my mother's prejudices, I never even tried to go to the Friday night dances in the gym, which were a good place to meet girls and mix socially. And I refused to go to Sunday School after we had moved. I think it was partly from bashfulness at meeting people close up and partly that I had begun going to church with my parents and really enjoyed it. First Presbyterian Church at that time had an English or Welsh minister, J.W.G. Ward. He had written some books, and he gave stimulating sermons. The church held close to one thousand people, I think; it was full on Sunday morning, and besides a good choir, it had a paid quartet of professional singers. (During part of this high-school period, my parents also kept up their membership in St. Paul's Union Church, which I had joined on Pearl Harbor Day, and we often drove the twenty miles to it on a Sunday morning.)

But if I did not make friends dancing or at church, I made enough of them at school to have a balanced life—or so I think. There was Jay Sweeney, who was on the *Tabula* board with me and in choir, and Joan Willens, a friend from Emerson days and (she says) my main competitor all throughout high school. We were in many classes together and frequently did our homework together on the phone. She came from a very well-regulated Jewish household and was also, in my opinion then, immensely wealthy. Because of the various musical affairs I was involved in, I was often at school until close to dinnertime, and it made up for any lack of intellectual stimulus at home. My piano playing culminated in my being the soloist with the high-school orchestra in my senior year: I played the first movement of the Rubinstein piano concerto.

Oak Park was nine miles from downtown Chicago. We lived between two elevated lines, each of which was a ten-minute walk and a thirty-minute trip to the Loop for ten cents. At twelve years of age, I was ready for the city. I do not remember going in all the time, but the city was "there" in a way it had not been when we lived in Beverly Hills. I frequently went to the movies downtown with my friends; by this time my mother's ban on movies had been effectively broken for me. During the war years, my parents and I also used to go to a newsreel-only movie downtown. This was one way of keeping up with the war—TV had not come into the home yet.

One could, I suppose, recollect enough to write an entire book about the high-school years. I do not remember ever thinking too much about where I would go to college—a phenomenon hard to believe today. Cookie interested me in the University of Chicago, and I knew its geography from singing in the choir a couple of times at Rockefeller Chapel or from going to the Oriental Institute. I also liked their Great Books or general education approach, and I think to this day that I did not get a very balanced liberal arts education at Harvard. But in my junior year I won the Harvard Book Award, a prize given to the top junior in many of the high schools where Harvard was looking for candidates. Local members of the Harvard Club of Chicago solicited me for Harvard and told me I would likely get a scholarship if I applied. I was a mid-year graduate from high school: That fate of being slightly misplaced in one's class had followed me ever since half of us had been promoted in the second grade in Chicago. I had half a year after commencement to wait for college and went to work as a bookkeeper in a local bank in Oak Park. I also did more socializing in that half year than I had ever done, since I was out of school and had no homework. I applied only to Harvard and do not remember being particularly anxious about hearing from them. In mid-April the announcements came, and I got both a Harvard College scholarship and some additional scholarship funds from the Harvard Club of Chicago. So a good part of my future in terms of the friends I would make, the experiences I would have for at least four years, the part of the country I would come to love, and even the woman I would marry hinged on a decision that I had made, if not casually, certainly without thought to all the events that would flow from it. (But is that really so unusual?)

Somewhere in here I wanted to mention the matter of being "smart." One time in high school I had inadvertently and wholly unintentionally seen my IQ score: I think it was 146. That is not genius, but it is smart. And it was the highest on the list I happened to see. Sometime toward the end of my high-school years the senior dean also told me, after we had taken a series of aptitude tests that I could literally succeed at anything I decided to do. I do not believe that my aptitude tests demonstrated any strong enough direction to be much of a guide. Knowing those things was a curse in a way. I have so far had a wonderful life, but knowing what my potential was, I cannot say that I consider myself particularly successful. I do not regret anything I have done, and it would not do much good if I did. But I do not feel there were any wrong turns, and I am particularly grateful that whatever success I had in the way of job recognition has been matched by feeling that we have had a wonderful marriage and a great family. Yet I know that a career that was extremely focused from Day One would have probably led to a greater success in some particular thing than anything else I have done. However, if even now I do not know what that focus might or should have been, what is the use of wondering?

When the war ended in August 1945, President Truman ended gasoline rationing within days. My father came home and said, "Let's go to Louisville." So we set off on our retread tires (the only tires civilian were driving at the end of the war) and drove at thirty-five mph all the way across Indiana. I think it took us almost twelve hours to go the three hundred miles. Louisville had a kind of mystique for me in those days. Once you were in southern Indiana, the pace changed, the accents changed, and then when you crossed the mile-long bridge over the Ohio River and entered Kentucky, it did not take much imagination to believe you had entered a different world. We drove, unannounced, to Doe and Wal's house. It was about dinnertime, and Wal was sitting out on the front porch in his swing. (We had thought he might be doing just that.) We drove up, and he hardly looked surprised. He said, "Well, I thought you might be coming along." He was the master of the understatement and in some ways similar to Walker LaBrunerie, my brother-in-law, in his lethargic temperament.

A year later, when I was considering Harvard, we made our first trip East, to Niagara Falls, upper New England, Boston and Cambridge, back down through New York and Washington. I did not have my mind too concentrated on college at that point, or I would have been more anxious about the trip. I remember seeing Boston more than Harvard, and I do not recall thinking that I would be back the next year.

* * * *

To go back to the 1930s: When I was growing up and largely playing by myself on Artesian Avenue, I had two imaginary friends. I have never known if these were mispronunciations of names I heard on the fifteen-minute radio serials that I listened to after school, but the names have never left me: Septedy Ongary and Septedy Brave. Do any of my cousins remember who they might have been?

* * * *

I have to treat the Harvard years as a unit. I went off to Harvard in the fall of 1947 and stayed for six years, except for coming home for EVERY vacation. Unlike many of my college friends, who either traveled or stayed at school at least during spring break, I traveled back to Chicago to visit my parents every time during those six years. It is difficult, without writing a whole book, to describe all that went on during those six years. I grew up, of course, in a way that any young man would between the ages of eighteen and twenty-four. I learned a lot academically, although college years are a combination of pleasure and pain. I thought I was in love with Kathy Franklin at times. She had come East to go to Wellesley, and I had gotten to know her during senior year at Oak Park, when she had returned from Japan, where her parents were missionaries. I am not sure she ever thought she was in love with me, but we did have many nice times together, and it was not an unpleasant relationship. It took up a lot of time, which was probably good, since I could not study or go to the movies all the time. I did not have a lot of close friends, but I made enough friends to satisfy my needs. Foremost among them, of course, were Walker LaBrunerie and Jim Drumwright, with whom I roomed during sophomore year and in whose suite I spent a good deal of my time during the last two years of college.

Early in my sophomore year I declared my major: history. It seemed an all-encompassing subject. I suppose the same could be said for philosophy or literature or even government, but history seemed to have it all. I may have made a mistake in specializing in American history, as I really did not know much about the rest of the world and in fact began to learn about it first-hand when I was in the Army later on. American history was really too specialized, when one considers how much there is to learn in a liberal arts education. Nevertheless, I enjoyed most of what I studied, and in my senior year I wrote a thesis on Octavius Brooks Frothingham, a minor figure in New England transcendentalism and Unitarianism (he had written a history of the former). Harvard was just beginning to have some core courses, which I "escaped" (unfortunately) by a year. I have thought in recent years that the best liberal arts course is like the original Chicago Great Books course or what is now done at the two St. Johns University campuses in Maryland and Santa Fe. The only exposure I had to science was one required course: Walker and I took Geology, otherwise known as Rocks. We did learn a lot about the glaciers and how the terrain around Boston was formed. We also heard our professor, Kirtley Mather, wax eloquent about Henry Wallace (this was during 1948, the year Wallace ran for President on a third-party ticket).

(Harvard deserves more attention, but since this is almost in the form of a bare outline of events, I must move on.)

The other important thing that happened to me at Harvard, beginning in 1947, was my interest in Christian Science. It must be clear from my discussion of my parents that religion and religious controversy were both strong elements in my background. During high-school days, my best friend was Jay Sweeney, whose mother was just entering the Christian Science practice. He came to Yale, and we saw each other frequently, especially during our first few years in the East. Then there were my cousins, Shirley and Paula. And to top it off, Kathy Franklin invited me to Thanksgiving dinner at the house of her parents' friends Ralph and Fannie Cessna. Ralph had been a Monitor correspondent, but had just moved East from Chicago to take a job with the religious periodicals. He was not yet a Christian Science practitioner. From that day onward, the Cessnas became friends of mine, whether Kathy was in the picture or not; after a year or so, she was usually not in it as far as they were concerned.

Exactly how I was drawn into Christian Science is not easy to say, since like many things in life it was a combination of factors. One was natural curiosity at being so close to the headquarters in Boston. One was admiration for literally everyone I had known up to that date who was a Scientist. During the summer of 1948 I began to read, surreptitiously at night, the Christian Science textbook that my father kept in the bookcase. It seemed to make sense. I was more interested in theological answers than in its healing message: Mrs. Eddy's respect for God, for the entire Christian tradition, but also her new words explaining what God can mean to us and her separation of the Christ from the human Jesus. I was ready to absorb such concepts. It is ironic, since it was the deep spirituality of her message that drew me in, and in many ways made me feel I was hearing my mother speak to me, that my mother was so bothered by my interest in Christian Science and many times said she would rather die than be healed by it. I would not go into this much detail in a short piece like this, except that this colored my relations with my parents for the rest of my Harvard years and usually made the trips back to Chicago painful, at least in part.

For most of the summers in Chicago, I worked as a bank teller at the Citizens National Bank. This bank was owned by largely the same set of directors who owned the National Bank of Commerce, where my father had worked since 1938. My Aunt Julia ran the safe deposit box area; we often ate our lunch together and went for a walk down Chicago Avenue. This arrangement did not make my mother particularly happy, as she apparently assumed I was getting more Christian Science from my aunt. Actually, Julia and Ray had wide-ranging intellectual interests; their lives in some respects were more like European intellectuals. They both took advantage of the art available in Chicago, in going, for instance, to a lot of the free lectures at the Art Institute. Also, for at least some of those summers, my cousin Shirley was at home; she had graduated from Grinnell College in 1948 and was working in Chicago.

As I approached graduation from Harvard in 1951, I was unsure about what my career would be. Many of my friends were going to law school—Harvard, naturally! I had taken the law-school aptitude tests and came out in the 99.5 percentile. I probably would have gotten major scholarship aid from the law school as a result. But I was unsure that I wanted to practice law, and to this day, I think that was a correct decision. The part of the law that interests me most are the large constitutional questions, but no one starting a career as one of several hundred thousand lawyers can plan that he will end up on a major juridical bench. My father encouraged me about the law. He had never intended to practice, either, but felt it was a good preparation for many kinds of work. Part of my thinking had to do with finances.

I knew it had been a challenge for my parents to keep me at Harvard, even though I had some scholarship aid all through college. My memory is that the last two years were not as substantial as the first two. And law school would have meant three more years.

As it was, I applied for a two-year terminal Master of Arts degree program in the Arts and Sciences faculty, an interdisciplinary program in International Studies. The program was geared for people who intended to take the foreign-service exam and presumably to follow a career in the foreign service. While I was at home on spring vacation, my roommate, Don Fox, wired me, "Congratulations - you hit the jackpot." I got a fellowship for, I believe, $2,000 a year. In any case, it came fairly close to paying for Harvard for the next two years. I took several government, history, and economics courses the first year, and it was in general like another year of college. But in the second year I did a paper that was not dissertation length, but involved substantial research, on the Institute of Pacific Relations, a Communist front organization that had recently been exposed. And I specialized in one area, the Islamic world, particularly Egypt, doing a paper on an educational reformer in the 1900-era. One also had to take a general oral exam to get the M.A. degree. I was examined by Dan Cheever, who ran the program; Rudolf Emerson, a distinguished older government professor; and a third person whom I forget. After the exam, I was told it had been "Ph.D. quality," and I wondered at times why I had not tried to go all the way in graduate study and get a doctorate.

I had not done graduate work just to stay out of military service. But the Korean War had begun the summer before my senior year in college, and everyone knew the draft awaited him as soon as he was out of school. Unlike World War II, draft deferments were quite common, and in the district I was registered in, the Chicago area, I had no problem getting deferred until 1953.

Before leaving Boston, though, there is one person I must mention who remained an influence on my life for the next thirty-five years: Gertrude Eiseman. In January 1949 I enrolled in The Mother Church Sunday School. I was nineteen years old, and Christian Science Sunday Schools are open to kids until they are twenty. I had gotten enough "into" Christian Science by that time that I wanted to see what I could get out of Sunday School. It is probably true, also, that Sundays in college are dismal, and going into Boston on Sunday morning with a purpose changed that. When I enrolled, I asked if I could have Erwin Canham as my teacher. He was the well-known editor of the Monitor, and I knew that he was popular with the college kids. But the superintendent, instead, told me that a woman by the name of Mrs. Eiseman was looking for a few students. Mrs. Eiseman at the time was about sixty; that seemed old to me. Moreover, she dressed conservatively, in a navy-blue dress. I assumed it was the same one every week, but it may not have been. I pictured her at first as a widow who did not have a lot, but loved her church, etc. As it turned out, Mrs. Eiseman was the widow of a wool merchant in Boston. He had been somewhat older, I believe, and had died in the early 1930s. The family was Jewish—her maiden name was Wechsler—and she told me once that she learned to speak German before English. She was raised in New York. Not only for the six months I had her as a teacher, but for the entire three and a half years I was still at Harvard, she stayed in touch. She lived in an apartment in the Vendome Hotel on Commonwealth Avenue and occasionally would have her Sunday School pupils over for dinner. During the time I was in the Army, she served a year as President of The Mother Church. This is a largely titular role, but one that is passed around only to people who have been of great service to the movement.

During my years at Harvard, my parents' living arrangements changed. We had lived at 524 Clinton Avenue, Oak Park, since 1941, with my grandparents. Marguerite now decided that it was time for her to take her turn, as it were, and wanted them to come and live with her. My mother was not eager to see them go, as they had been good companionship for her, especially since I had been away at college. But they moved sometime in 1951, and in the spring of 1952, Mom and Dad bought a house on the edge of LaGrange at 6929 Willow Springs Road. It was only a few years old, but not particularly well built. My father liked it because he had a half-acre yard to work in. Gardening had long been his main recreation, and the small yard in Oak Park, with little privacy, was not enough for him. His commute was much worse, but he did not seem to mind that. It was not a thoughtful move if one considered my mother, however. She did not drive a car and never wanted to learn. She was virtually housebound, although she could walk two blocks to highway 66 and catch a commuter bus to go into downtown Chicago. But she had no way to go just a few miles to the shops in LaGrange. All in all, in retrospect, it seems like a move that they did not think out very well.

Just before answering my draft call, I had class instruction in Christian Science with Ralph Cessna. He had been made a Christian Science teacher the year before, after moving from Boston back to Chicago. The class lasts for two weeks. Toward the end of the first week, I called my father at the bank from Evanston and was told rather mysteriously to call home. I called home to find that my grandmother, aged ninety, had fallen the day before and died the same day in a hospital. The funeral was to be on a Saturday, so I interrupted my class period with a visit home and went to the funeral over the weekend.

On September 29, 1953, I became a soldier—US55435956. We were shipped out to Fort Riley, Kansas, where our company must have had the roughest set of NCOs any company going through basic training ever had. They were Korean vets, and they were taking it out on us young guys who were not going to have to fight. We were forced to call them "sir" until, toward the end of basic training, someone complained up the line and that nonsense was stopped. I weighed 140 pounds when I went in the Army, and within less than a year I was up to 160 pounds. So something about the regimen was not all bad. Most of the guys I was in basic with were either working-class guys from Chicago or farmers from the Middle West. I learned and heard more about sex in those few months than I had leared or heard at Harvard. I also saw how diverse we are as a nation. There were several guys who had been in business for themselves as farmers for several years already, and for them taking two years out for military service was more of a problem than for me. I did not know what I was going to do when I got out anyhow!

When basic training was over, just before Christmas, I asked about enrolling in the Counter Intelligence Corps. I did not want to waste the entire two years and had heard that there was more interesting work there. I was told that they had already picked a few for that and had ignored me because I did not have the top physical profile. I think the profiles had six grades, and I was in the second just because I wore glasses. But they looked at my record and said if I would re-enlist, for three years, I could go to CIC school. Between possibly wasting two years and giving away an extra year of my life to the Army, I decided to gamble on what the extra year would bring. And that is how another of life's choices got made—not exactly by accident, but also not with a lot of forethought.

I had a leave at Christmas and came back to Kansas just before New Year's. We got off New Year's Eve afternoon, and

I decided to join Walker and Kathie LaBrunerie in St. Joe (St. Joseph, Missouri). Kathie was working at the Harvard Business School. Walker was in a combined four-year Russian studies and Law School program at Harvard. It was a bitter winter evening, and after getting a ride from someone from Fort Riley to Kansas City, I stood on a hill in downtown Kansas City waiting for the bus to St. Joe. When I got to St. Joe, late in the evening, Walker picked me up, and we went to the Rositzkys' house, where a New Year's Eve party was in progress. I ended up playing the piano, and I remember Kathie leaning against it, wearing a black dress and holding a glass of champagne; I felt as if I had "come home" at last. And I had, for that was the evening from which I have to date everything that has happened since!

I have not mentioned Kathie before this, but we had known each other since 1948, when she transferred from Missouri University to Smith College. She does not remember the incident, but I have often told her about the Friday evening when Walker and I and probably some other people had been to the movies and ended up at the Howard Johnson's in Harvard Square. He said his sister and a friend, Mary Shaw, were coming to Cambridge for the weekend, and while we were sitting there, they came walking down the steps to find us, or rather, Walker. Kathie was a fairly frequent weekend visitor and had become a good friend. I think I confided in her about some of my problems with other girls, including Kathy Franklin. But she was also dating Jim Drumwright part of this time, and our relationship was simply one of being friends. (As I now know how the French would describe it, she was *ma copine*, not *ma petite amie*.) She graduated from Smith in 1950 and worked in St. Joe for two years, for the Chamber of Commerce and for a radio station planning popular music programs.

In the spring of 1952, halfway between my two M.A. years, she and Walker and I took Pierre Falquet, a Frenchmen studying at Harvard that year, down to New Orleans and to some of the famous Southern towns in Mississippi. Then she came back to Boston to look for a job, ending up at the Business School. The spring she came back she was boarding at the house next to Professor Demos's, where Walker and I shared the third floor. Many mornings she came over for breakfast with me, which I think consisted mainly of orange juice and coffee. I loved her company, but the relationship still went no farther at the time. But during the 1952-53 school year (my last), I saw more of her, and when I went into the Army I began to realize how much I missed her company. But if I am to be as honest as my memory will let me be, I think that when I went over to St. Joe that New Year's Eve I was not going for more than a good night away from the Army to be enjoyed with both Walker and Kathie. The next day, however, we went for a long walk. New Year's had gotten much warmer, as it can out there, and as we walked I began to talk to her in terms I had not used before this. I was to have a leave before starting CIC school, and the idea came to me to start driving to Boston and see how far I could get in a week. I had never borrowed our one and only car before, and I do not remember how I approached my father. And it must have been a hardship for him to be without it for a week or more. But I drove to Boston, we were together every evening, and at the end of my four or five days in Boston, when we informed him that we were going to get married, Walker, in his usual lethargic manner, replied, "Are you sure you know what you're doing?"

Early in March I reported to CIC school at Fort Holabird, Baltimore, Maryland. The next four months were some of the happiest months of my entire life, even though they were also very stressful. Learning the elements of counterespionage was a new world for me. Unlike basic training, I was with guys who were more nearly from my background; in many cases, we really enjoyed each other's company. Dick Murphy, who had a distinguished career in the U.S. Foreign

Service, was in my group, for instance. It was a stressful period for two reasons: first, the McCarthy hearings were about to start, and second, the fear spread abroad by Senator McCarthy was much on my mind. Somewhere in this period I had sent a letter to the Monitor criticizing the Eisenhower administration for not taking any action against McCarthy. The letter had been published, and I began to fear that someone might connect it with my being trained at Holabird and that I would be ferreted out of the program. (We were all being investigated before being given top-secret clearances.)

The other stressful element was that I went to Boston every weekend but one for the next three months. A fellow in my class was an accountant in Maine and tried to go home every weekend to keep his business going. We would leave Holabird at noon on Saturday, driving the 350-plus miles to Boston. Kathie would pick me up in Wellesley Hills about seven in the evening. We would have Saturday night together and Sunday. At 7:00 P.M Sunday this fellow would pick me up again in Wellesley, and we would get into Baltimore about 2:30 A.M. It took all of Monday to feel alive again, and I would tell Kathie I was not coming the next weekend. By Wednesday I would have changed my mind, and we were off to Boston again on Saturday.

But it was springtime, I was in love, and of course I could not wait to get away from "spy school" after a tense week there. When I think that our children have done some things that did not seem safe or wise, I need to remember those months. Once we were pulled over on the New Jersey Turnpike; the cop said we were doing ninety mph, although I think it was not quite that bad. After he saw that we were in uniform, he let us go without even a written warning.

Because we had decided to marry on fairly short notice, Kathie's mother could not book the St. Joseph Country

Club for a weekend night in June. Hence we got married on June 29, a Tuesday. I was not even sure a few months prior whether I could be there! But I knew CIC graduation was set for the Friday before June 29, and I assumed I could work it out. And Kathie's mother simply said, "Well, just tell your commanding officer you have to go to your wedding." I flew home to Chicago on June 26, went to the dentist, and on Sunday the 27th my parents and I drove to St. Joe. The weather was beastly hot. In St. Joe we had to go to parties Sunday evening, lunch on Monday, and a big family party at the LaBruneries' on Monday evening. On Tuesday the temperature rose to 102 degrees, and the candles in the church melted. There was a big reception at the country club, and late in the evening, Ted, the black man who worked for them, delivered our car to us, all packed with the things we needed for six months in California.

When we had first gotten our orders for post-CIC, I had been given orders to go to Japan. It was difficult, if not actually forbidden, at the time for an enlisted man to take his wife to Japan. My mother was recovering from electric shock treatments (more about her below), and I knew my leaving just then would be very difficult for my father, who had suffered probably more than she from her mental illness. I do not remember the actual coincidence of circumstances that changed my assignment. But early on I had indicated that I would like to be sent to the Army Language School to learn German. In fact, one inducement to signing up for three years had been the possibility that I could learn a foreign language. At the same time, my mother's psychiatrist had written a letter stating the circumstances of her illness and requesting that I not have to go abroad so soon. Anyhow, there had been no assignments to the language school for several months. Then Fred Spotts, whom I had gotten to know in the Christian Science Organization at Harvard in the 1952-53 year (he was studying at the Fletcher School at Tufts), came to tell me that he heard they had just gotten two billets for Monterey. We skipped our classes that morning and sat in the Army's personnel office pleading our case. The result was that, of all the men in our group, we were the only two sent to language school. (I was also the honor student in our graduating class, although I do not know if the personnel people would have known who was going to get that award before the actual graduation week.)

* * * *

Before continuing my story, which now becomes the joint story of Kathie and me, I need to pick up a bit about my mother, whose illness I have referred to above. She had always been a highly sensitive and insecure person; but other than that, she was normally sociable (although wanting to avoid too much contact with people whose views she did not agree with). But sometime in the fall of 1951, after my grandparents had moved out of our house in Oak Park, she began to tell my father stories about some of the men at the local grocery store flirting with her. The store was owned by Italians, and she had a particularly hard time dealing with Italians and Catholics. What may have happened is that a delivery man made some harmless complimentary remark about how nice she looked. She was a natural blond and had a lovely smile. Then she began to think people were spreading stories about her, etc. It took a while for us to tumble to what was going on, and I do not think I was made aware of all this until I came home for Christmas vacation that year. But it was a full-blown attack of paranoia. I do not remember the actual progression of events or the date when all the relatives were informed or became aware of her troubles. The situation continued on through 1952 after they had moved to LaGrange, and I believe it was only in the winter of 1952-53 that my father finally convinced her to see a psychiatrist. Although she never accepted the claim about her illness, she did finally consent to having shock treatment. My aunt Julia accompanied her to the sessions; I believe there were two a week for several weeks. When I came home for my last spring break from Harvard I was concerned about my father. The ordeal had been difficult for him, and his unusual flushed color probably indicated some kind of developing heart trouble.

Mother never really improved. Dr. Sadler, the psychiatrist, was at the time a fairly elderly man and held in high esteem in Chicago. He said that her troubles stemmed from her views of sex and religion. But merely identifying that did not, of course, explain why she may have had certain views or why, when I am sure they were shared by millions of other persons of her generation and background, they did not make other people ill. Her illness ended whatever social intercourse they had had, and I think it made my father love his garden even more. Ray and Jul also saved his life, as he could confide in them. In the years that he had left, after Ray and Julia had taken an apartment together in Oak Park, he frequently paid short calls on them going to work or coming home. The shock therapy destroyed my mother's short-term memory, which did not increase her comfort level! At some point, I also suggested to my father, with not much thought about the consequences, that it would be better for him if he could place her in a sanatorium. In the first place, I do not think he could consider such a thing financially, but I realized that he also took his marriage vows seriously and that he would never even consider that solution as an alternative. As long as she was not placed in situations where she could imagine some new deviltry being planned against her, life at home could continue more or less normally. When it came to our wedding in 1954, she would not have been comfortable socially with most of Kathie's parents' associates anyhow. She was fairly silent at all the wedding festivities, but carried things off well.

I hope (I am saying this to whoever reads this some day) that I have not been unfair to my mother's memory. It should be obvious that I felt exceptionally close to my father all my life. He was a rare person, and I still have trouble keeping the tears back whenever I think of him. But he could also be impatient at times, and I realize in retrospect that we all share some of the blame as well as some of the praise for how the lives of those around us turn out. Temperamentally, he and my mother may not have been suited for each other, although that certainly was not clear to them in the 1920s or in the delightful doggerel verses my mother would write to him when they were engaged. Somehow my mother became overly rigid and was inclined to judge other people harshly when they did not measure up to her views of what was right. But she could also be very sweet, and people who did not know of her paranoia might be surprised to know about this aspect of her life. I do not think that our children, whom she visited with many times until her death in 1980, were ever aware at the time that she had mental problems.

* * * *

To continue: We were married on June 29. We drove, in five days, to San Francisco via Kearney, Nebraska; Cheyenne, Wyoming; Salt Lake City; Carson City; and finally, on July 4, we reached San Francisco. I was unprepared for California, although I had been told that at the presidios of San Francisco and Monterey the Army never issued summer uniforms. We had come down from Lake Tahoe early on the afternoon of July 4. First of all, I was unprepared for "gold and green" California—the grass on the mountainsides had already turned brown, but the hillsides were dotted with those fabulous live oak trees. Then we came to Sacramento and walked around the Capitol in steamy heat. So it was a shock, when we came over the low hills surrounding San Francisco Bay to the town of Richmond, to be greeted by what seemed to be about a fifty mph wind. We spent the next day or two touring San Francisco. Then on to Monterey, where I reported in, and we went in search of a house. We found a small beach cottage just a block from the Pacific Ocean, 502 Asilomar Boulevard, and this was our home, our first, for the next six months.

The routine at the Army Language School was the same every day: three hours of instruction in the morning, a break from about 11:00 A.M. until 1:00 P.M., and three more hours in the afternoon. We had six different instructors: a Herr Becker who had been a Nazi soldier and was still a racist; a cute young woman who was supposed to have been a Communist, but had slept with enough of the "right" soldiers to get a visa; a Herr Rosenfeld, a very intellectual German Jew; Werner Sewald, who was the least German—he had lived in America since 1929, etc. No grammar as such was taught; it all had to be by example. I would drive to the presidio in the morning and come home for lunch. Then Kathie would take me in the afternoon and do errands or window-shop in Carmel; she would pick me up at 4:00 P.M., and we would often go sit on the beach in Carmel. The weather was idyllic, but not what we were used to in summer. During July and August there is a lot of fog on the Monterey coast, and for about five weeks we had little sunshine at all unless we drove inland about five miles. The temperature varied from about 55 degrees at night to 65 in the daytime. It was a bit disappointing at times not to have summer heat and the sense of relaxation that can go with it. But we found we both loved the moderate temperature, and of course the terrain and the Monterey pines and the cypresses made this one of the most beautiful sites I had yet seen. For years I had a sort of goal to somehow get back to Carmel to live and work. It might not have been a bad idea, but it never turned out that way. In the years since, we have visited it often: twice while we lived in Phoenix in the early 1960s and many times since 1980. It has changed and not all for the better. But it is still one of the most beautiful spots on earth, and even Carmel village has been pretty well protected.

Those months were Uncle Sam's gift to us for our honeymoon. We were away from our families, although Katherine and Walker visited us in August, and my parents and Ray and Doe came for Thanksgiving. But this was our first time to really be alone, and it was a wonderful base from which to build the rest of our lives. I was not thankful enough to Uncle Sam at the time, however, as I chafed at the thought of having "given away" three years of my life. Fred Spotts became a lifelong friend. We made two other close friends in Roy Alexander and Gordon Johnson, and we kept in touch with both of them until the mid-1980s.

In December my orders came to go to Germany, and we proceeded East via Yosemite National Park; a night in Phoenix, where the skies were the clearest I had ever seen; and St. Joseph and Chicago. We ended up in Boston, and Kathie came down with me to New York when I had to report to Fort Dix. I sailed on January 29 or 30, and she returned to Boston for a few weeks.

Our journey to Europe was interrupted by our having to stand by a disabled freighter for three days, as our own boat rocked back and forth. Fred Spotts and I had become the editors of the ship's newspaper. We were both slightly uncomfortable the first two days out of New York, but we adjusted well after that. When we finally left the freighter behind after it got other help, I was as surprised as I had been by the cold air of northern California to see the south coast of England, on about the tenth of February, and the fields all a bright spring green. We disembarked at Bremerhaven, after a slow approach from the North Sea up the channel into Bremerhaven harbor. A band on shore played some American music to welcome us, but it had the opposite effect on me. We were sent by train to a transfer station somewhere in the Saar, and from there Fred and I were sent to Stuttgart, the headquarters of the 66th CIC. There we had our first practice in using the German we had been learning. I remember our going to the Christian Science church there—Fred was still a Scientist at this point. The reading in English was stiff, but he commented that they deserved credit for trying. Fred got sent to Berlin, where only single men were sent by the CIC, and I was given orders for Frankfurt, or rather, Offenbach, a town upriver on the Main from Frankfurt. Meanwhile, Kathie had sailed on the S.S. *United States*, and my commanding officer gave me orders to proceed to Bremerhaven to meet her. One of my distinct memories of that early period is the train ride to the port. Most of it was at night, although a good part of the day is night at that time of the year. In town after town, as the train glided through, Germans would be out walking, looking in the store windows. Everything was so peaceful; it was hard to reconcile what I was seeing with what had been going on there only ten years earlier.

The CIC had several missions. Perhaps the largest number of personnel were engaged in doing background checks on people who wanted to work for the Army. There was a counterespionage unit. Then there was a countersubversion unit, a relic from the early Cold War days when the Army had had some fear that the Communist Party in Germany would try to subvert the U.S. mission. I believe it had been started a year or two after the end of the war. In any case, CIC had several contacts within the Communist Party, and some of them had risen to fairly high posts. The party itself had become largely a debating society, and its threat to the occupation was minimal. But occasionally one could learn something that might have intelligence interest in Heidelberg or Washington when tied in with information from other sources. I was assigned two or three "sources," each with a numbered code name, and I would meet with them, usually once a week, to hear what they had to say and to get written information from them. The rest of the week would be spent in the office translating whatever documents I had received. It was good practice for my written German.

At first Kathie and I lived in a rented room in an apartment owned by a Frau Stockhausen. We had use of the bedroom, a balcony, and the bath. The toilet in the hall we shared. Frau Stockhausen had the most intelligent black poodle we have ever known, and Kathie would let him in in the morning after he had had his run on the street. The apartment was at 47 Kronbergerstrasse in the West End. I have visited the neighborhood many times in recent years. It appears to be a building that had been built in the 1920s or 1930 and had probably suffered negligible war damage. About eighty percent of the housing in Frankfurt was destroyed or damaged severely, and there were still many housing units that had not been restored. However, the West End was one of the most desirable areas of Frankfurt, and we could walk into the center of the city in about fifteen minutes. We were also close to the former Farben headquarters, which was all U.S. Army. The first year I worked out of the Offenbach field office, but most of the second year David Lansing and I shared an office in the Farben building. By that time we were living in Eschenheim, at the northern tip of the then boundary of Frankfurt.

The first Fourth of July we were there, a friend, Peter Van Pelt, invited us to a party at his house. To my surprise I found a copy of the Christian Science Lesson Sermon in their bedroom, and it turned out that his wife, Patricia, was a Christian Scientist. The Van Pelts became close friends and remain so to this day. About a month after this party, Peter was transferred to France, and we were able to take over their house. It was the last house in a group of eight row houses. The rent was 400DM per month, about $100, or about half my pay as a private. It was decently furnished, had central heat with the coal "oven" in the kitchen, and a marvelous grand piano. The owner's husband, who had committed suicide in the basement, had been a pianist and had left behind a great collection of classical music. The house made all the difference for the eighteen or so months we still lived in Germany. We had several bachelor friends to dinner frequently. I played the piano almost daily. David Lansing, who became one of our closest friends, came to dinner frequently, and he and Kathie would sit discussing obscure European royalty and their connections while I played my Beethoven. The living room looked out on a garden. Kathie took down the gauzy curtain that covered the picture windows and put up two pink sheets, which transformed the room and horrified the owner of the house. CIC agents in Berlin were required to come out of Berlin on a sealed train, so every time Fred Spotts had a leave, he would come through Frankfurt on the night train. We would discuss our current views of the Germans; we were usually at about the same stage of development.

As any journalist will tell you, when you enter a new culture you quickly make an assessment. Then, as time goes on, you are required to make adjustments to that assessment. You begin to see life from the others' point of view. You learn more about how their history, their climate, and their economy shaped their thinking. And there is the fact that in your own interaction with the other culture, you are changed by it; but you also cannot resist imposing your deepest views on your assessment of it. In the end, you probably come out with a judgment that is remarkably like the one you first made, but with ever so many caveats to qualify it. And that was what I found remarkable about the way in which Fred and I seemed to react to what we were seeing.

Because I was in the "spy" business, I did not have to wear an Army uniform. In fact, I was given a generous clothing allowance and kept a German tailor busy making me suits for a few months. They were all made of fine English woolens, and unfortunately, too heavy for the way we heat houses in America. But they were fine while I was in Germany. Incidentally, in the first year of our marriage, my weight had gone up another twenty pounds, from 160 pounds to 180. It has remained within a few pounds of that for almost fifty years now. But first the Army and then married life - and Kathie's cooking - shaped me up. I cannot imagine what I must have looked like at 140 pounds!

One person who had a role in our life during this period was Rosa Marti. Marti was the youngest, I think, of eleven children in a Swiss family. She had emigrated to America in 1935 and become a U.S. citizen just before the war. She knew six or seven languages and worked as a censor for the U.S. government during the war. When the war ended, she came to Europe with the Army of Occupation. She joined CIC early on, and when the countersubversion unit was founded to follow the activities of the Communist Party, she became one of the chief behind-the-scenes record keepers. She had a 5 x 7 card file on everyone who was anyone in the KPD. Because she was a walking encyclopedia and also because of her linguistic abilities, there was usually a line of us agents at her desk asking her questions. We saw her socially as well. She had become interested in Christian Science in America, and her hero in the CIC was Bill Rohkam, a Christian Scientist from Beverly Hills. Bill had graduated from Stanford Law School in the late 1930s, was in the Army during the war, and stayed on for a while as a civilian worker. I think she became interested in us partly because I was a Christian Scientist. But she also loved Kathie.

Marti had a love-hate relationship with America. She was glad she had become a citizen, but said she would never want to live here. During Christmas in 1950, she and a French woman friend who also worked for CIC had bought a small house with five acres of land between Grasse and Cannes for $5,000. (More about this when I get to 1970.)

She intended to retire there when her working days were finished. She also had an enduring (and, for us, endearing) attitude toward the Army brass, which made all of us non-officer agents appreciate her. One day when I was complimenting her on her vast sum of knowledge about the KPD, she answered, "*Dans le royaume des aveugles, les borgnes sont rois.*" (In the kingdom of the blind, the one-eyed are kings.)

For a good part of the two years we lived in Frankfurt, I was hoping I would get an early discharge from the Army. While I certainly had very interesting work to do, considering that it was the peacetime Army, I was frustrated at not being able to get on with my life. In retrospect, of course, we *were* getting on with our lives, and in some ways the total Army experience added to my education in a way the university could not have done. I had to get used to so many kinds of people, I had the challenge and opportunity to use a foreign language, and we got to travel over an extended period in Europe. Unlike tourists doing the Grand Tour, we saved our leave time and used it in big enough chunks to do major trips to France in the summer of 1955; to Holland in the spring of 1956; several shorter trips to Switzerland; a trip to Bavaria and Austria in the fall of 1955, just after the Russians had pulled out of Vienna; and finally, a trip to Italy with my uncle Ray in November 1956. This was at the end of the Hungarian Revolution, and for several days we had not known if it would result in the next war. Kathie's parents had sent her the money to fly home if necessary. By the time we went to Italy with Ray, I believe the threat of a war had vanished. But the church bells in Milan and Venice still tolled in memory of the Hungarians who had been killed during the revolt. We also visited France several other times in that period and took innumerable day trips in western Germany and some overnight trips to Bavaria and Salzburg.

I grew increasingly negative about the Germans. At first I had admired the normal way they seemed to be living, only ten years after such a destructive war—destructive to their physical environment and just as upsetting to their mental equilibrium to go through such a period of oppression, even if many of them did admire Hitler in the early years. But I got tired of their alleged bullheadedness. Marti said she had never known an American of German extraction who did not come to feel this way about the Germans. I do not know yet how to account for it. During this same period, West Germany formally regained its sovereignty, and this may have made some of the populace a bit less tolerant of the huge American presence. In any case, that attitude did not persist throughout the rest of my life: Beginning in 1967, when I went back to Europe every year, I admired the progress the Germans had made. I also had a chance in later years to make many friendships with Germans on a personal level that were not possible while I was a "spion" in their midst.

Over the Labor Day weekend in 1955, Kathie had a miscarriage. We had known she was pregnant for several weeks. She had been very pale and was often lying out in the garden when I would come home. The doctor said it was probably an imperfect fetus, etc., that that was often why a miscarriage resulted. I do not know if that is true, but in any case, it set us both back for several months. Until a couple have produced a baby, they are never sure they can do it, and the uncertainty caused by the miscarriage left a question mark hanging in our minds.

Late in the fall of 1956 I received orders to fly home at the end of December. This meant that I would actually get out of the Army two or three months earlier than the three years for which I had re-enlisted. My memory is that only married men were being flown home; single men were still going on troop ships. I had to take my car, our 1952 Ford, to Bremerhaven about the middle of December so it could be shipped back to New York. Then Ray, who had traveled somewhere else after our November trip to Italy, joined us in Frankfurt for the holidays. The night after Christmas the Schwarzes had us over for supper, and years later Arnold Schwarz would remind me how much my uncle liked his German wine. The Schwarzes were a couple (she was Scottish) who had befriended Kathie early on in our stay in Eschersheim, and we kept in touch with them until they died. The nights for a couple of days in December were unusually foggy. We left our house, I believe, on December 28 and stayed at Rhein-Main air base. Our flight was delayed one day because of the fog, and we finally left on the night of December 30. David Lansing came to see us while we were waiting. We flew from Frankfurt to Shannon, Ireland, in four hours. After refueling, we flew another ten hours to Gander, Newfoundland. I will always remember the tears that came to my eyes when I saw the snowy mountains of Newfoundland and realized I was back in North America. In fact, to this day, after crossing the Atlantic at least one hundred times if one counts both directions, I still experience some kind of emotional jolt when I first sight some part of North America. I suspect it has something to do with remembering how I felt after returning from those two years abroad.

We landed in New York (Kennedy airport was then called Idlewild) after another four-hour flight from Newfoundland. It was mid-morning, December 31, and I was told to fetch my car early, since it was New Year's Eve. The car had arrived, and we were housed at Ft. Hamilton in Brooklyn. Kathie's Uncle Henry took us to an early New Year's Eve dinner in Manhattan that night, and we both thought the waiters were crude and rude after the kind of professional service we had become used to in Europe. Thus began our readjustment to a U.S. that in many ways we had forgotten. This was the era of the tail-fin cars, often painted in two colors. But we loved the sunshine. New Year's Day was bright, and we had forgotten how dim the sun is in northern

Europe for months on end. I was finally discharged on January 3, 1957, and we drove to Boston. We stayed with the Newmans, saw Walker, and I went to *The Christian Science Monitor* to start my job search.

I had been spared from making any firm decision about a career by the knowledge that I had to do my military service. I had taken an M.A. degree in International Studies at Harvard with the thought that I might take the Foreign Service exam and follow that as a career if I were accepted. After experiencing the bureaucracy of the Army, that thought had gradually left me. Some of the CIA employees in the Farben building had approached me informally to see if I would care to transfer over from CIC to them, but any more time in the spy business did not appeal at all. I suspect that I was also impatient to get on with a career and felt that the foreign-service ladder did not offer enough opportunity. I have already commented that some basic choices seem to get made without a tremendous amount of forethought. On the other hand, there is a kind of background thought that plays a significant role and makes a decision more understandable. In my case, I believe I had always felt the effects of growing up in relatively modest circumstances. I knew about my father's turn of affairs in the Depression; earning a decent living was more important to me than it may be to our family today. Through her letters, Kathie's mother exerted a fair amount of pressure on me to become financially successful, although that element in isolation certainly did not explain my decisions.

One of the ways I had considered of being involved in public affairs was to write for the Monitor. I admired Erwin Canham, the editor, and Ralph Cessna, who was my teacher in Christian Science, was a former Monitor staffer, mainly having been the Chicago bureau chief during the 1930s. During the time in Germany, I had written several vignettes about aspects of life in Germany that I thought might be useful on the Home Forum page. I had submitted them; they had all been rejected, politely. Since we were on the East Coast now, I had decided it would be the right time to see about starting out on a career in journalism. I had gotten an appointment with Canham through John Hoagland, the manager (read publisher) of The Christian Science Publishing Society. Hoagland had gotten involved because I had written to the Hurleys (Tom was a Director of the church) that I might be interested. I spent an interesting few hours at the Monitor, but Canham said they had no openings at the moment, and when they did, copyboys started at fifty dollars a week. Since I have already mentioned my impatience about "getting ahead," and since journalism was not actually a burning desire, that ended my attempt to work for the Monitor—then! A few days later we started out for Chicago, for a reunion with my parents. By this time it also looked as if Kathie might be pregnant again.

One of the memories we both have of returning to the U.S. is that all of our parents had become fatter! They were roughly in their sixth decade, none of them got much exercise, and they probably ate too much. My parents usually had a box of chocolates in the living room, and although they did not gorge themselves, that habit had probably helped add a couple of pounds. We also thought my parents' house was too hot. We had grown used to a cool house, first in our cottage in Pacific Grove that had virtually no heat, and then in our apartment in Frankfurt.

I thought that perhaps I could get a job in banking, as a way to get a good business education in general. I certainly had no clear career goal in mind at that moment. As the weeks went by, I was more excited over the likelihood that we would become parents that year. We were both somewhat apprehensive over Kathie's pregnancy at first, remembering the experience she had had in Frankfurt. While we were visiting in St. Joe, I had talks with two banks in Kansas City:

Billy Kemper was chairman of the largest bank there and a fraternity brother of Kathie's father; Kathie's uncle, Ford Nelson, ran the trust department at the First National Bank. At least at the First, I think I would have had a job offer if I had pursued it. We returned to Chicago (or perhaps I went up alone), and I interviewed at The Northern Trust Company, where I was hired as a credit analyst. On March 15, when Kathie was probably ten or eleven weeks pregnant, she came to Chicago on the train, and we began to look for an apartment. I had thought at first that we would live in Evanston. The commuting was good, and this was where so many young professionals lived. I also felt that having grown up in Oak Park I had not experienced the real feel of Chicago—that is, either in living close to downtown or living on the Michigan shore. However, the old apartments had no charm, and at some point, we decided to try to buy a modest house. I had also made the decision to stay in Chicago awhile partly out of concern for my father. Millie had written to me, or to someone who told me, that it would take a lot of burden off my father if I were around some. Whether in the end I lifted any burden from him is questionable, as I remember myself being mainly impatient with getting ahead, etc. But the decision to be near my parents eventually made us concentrate our looking in the southwestern suburbs along the Burlington Railroad, which had good commuting.

We bought a house at 4610 Woodland Avenue in Western Springs, four or five miles from my parents' house, and two blocks from the railroad station. I set to work seriously and took accounting courses at night at the University of Chicago's downtown campus. It was the beginning of my post-college education, which in one form or another continues until today. How did we manage to buy a house? It cost $18,500, and I got a loan for $13,500. I believe my father gave us a thousand dollars, and Nana LaBrunerie, my grandmother-in-law, gave us most of the rest, with Kathie's parents contributing the difference. If we had known we would be living there for only a bit more than a year, we would probably not have purchased it. We worked hard to make the house more pleasant, within our limited budget, and Kathie's mother sent us some furniture. We also had unpacked our wedding presents, which we had not really savored until this time, and they created a sense of luxury far beyond our means at the time.

We were in Chicago only from March 1957 until the end of the summer of 1958. The main event of the period was the birth of Ann on September 5. My parents had come by to see us the evening before; it was still about a week from Kathie's due date. Later that evening she began to go into labor, and we went to the hospital at about our normal bedtime. Ann was born at seven in the morning, and I rushed home to phone my parents. My father was out working in his garden, as he did all summer before going to work, and my mother yelled the news to him. He asked, "Was it a boy?" I do not remember then, or at any of the other births, though, ever wishing that it would be one sex or the other. Maybe there is a sense of completeness that a parent feels when he or she has both sexes, but every individual is unique, and the role a father plays in bringing them into being is so capricious that it is the height of egotism to feel that one has to clone oneself to be complete. Anyway, Ann was a beautiful baby. Kathie was kept in the hospital for five days, and when she came home, Katherine, her mother, came to help for a week or so. We also had a nurse for some of the time, partly to teach Kathie what to do with the baby! We were just staring to learn that parenting is, from start to finish, an amateur job.

At my first anniversary, my salary was raised from $5300 to $5800, and I was told this was a good raise. I was not actually sure, but I knew I was learning on the job. The Northern liked to say it had the best MBA program in Chicago. Many of the guys there went on to work in smaller banks that were correspondents of the Northern, and they knew they would not keep all the trainees. At the same time, Katherine worked on us to come down to St. Joe so I could work with Kathie's father, Walker Sr. I never knew for sure if he really wanted a son-in-law working with him. But in August 1958 he became ill and went out to Colorado for a rest. This was unlike him. Amid the concern about his health and Katherine's urging, I decided rather quickly to make the move to St. Joe. Kathie was never that keen to go, as she knew the limitations of the town. I was also interested in being a serious Christian Scientist and had joined the church in Hinsdale. We also saw the Cessnas frequently, and I believe that Ralph was somewhat hesitant about my working with the family—although I do not think he ever tried to overtly influence my decision. As for Christian Science, I do not think I ever thought through the possible family disagreements that might result if I became heavily involved in a Christian Science church in St. Joe. Nevertheless, we came to St. Joe early in August 1958 and began the second of two rather short periods of my career.

No sooner had we arrived in St. Joe than it became evident that Walker needed more than a rest. He came back from Colorado sicker than when he went, and after some tests at the University of Kansas hospital in Kansas City, he was diagnosed as having a malignant brain tumor. He endured a successful operation, but it was a kind of cancer that spreads throughout the body, and he was given a very negative prognosis, something to the effect that he had just lived the best day he would ever have. He was in and out of the hospital throughout the fall and winter, although he was nursed at home more than in the hospital. At the same time, his parents, Nana, in her eighties, and Papa, who was ninety-one, became frantic over the situation. Nana would call me at the office, sometimes several times during the day. I did not always know how to react; she was forgetful, and in any case, the whole family had come to look on the office as their private fiefdom. Papa still came down every day and took out his safe deposit box to look at his stock certificates.

As for my work, I fitted into that very easily. First Federal S&L was in the home loan business. I had accompanied my father on weekends when he would make inspections of housing under construction that the bank was financing. So I was used to the elements of construction. The other part of the job, taking loan applications for mortgages, came quickly, and I also sometimes waited on customers at the window. There were only five or six employees in a $10 million operation. Walker did not take out much in the way of salary, but he insisted on writing all the homeowners' insurance. I learned the landscape of St. Joe very quickly and realized what a backwater the town had become. I also began to feel that, no matter what I did, I would for a long time be identified mainly as "Walker's son-in-law."

One bright spot was that Walker Jr. had started in the practice of law in Kansas City, and we saw him frequently. After Walker Sr. died, as well as the grandparents, he was involved in settling all three estates, so that assured we would see him frequently.

Just before he had become ill, Walker Sr. had built a modern bank building out on the Belt Highway and, the very week we moved down from Chicago, moved a small country bank that he owned into St. Joe. He did this without the government's approval, which assuredly would have been denied. There were nine banks in St. Joe at the time, and the town was regarded as over-banked. The Monday after the bank opened at its new location, the bank examiners arrived, probably intent on closing us down. I told them I was glad to see them, which they probably did not believe. Anyway, the bank was run prudently, so there were no immediate grounds to close us down for being unsafe, and the matter dragged on for over a year. Walker Jr. and I flew to

Washington during the winter to present our "case" before the FDIC, one of whose members was from Missouri. He assured us privately that something would be worked out, but on the surface the government proceeded as if we would be shut down. After Walker Sr. died the government moved. They told us the bank was under-capitalized and that funds must be added to the capital. This took a good part of the liquid funds that the estate was able to mobilize, but we put in the money and the bank got permission to stay in business. A few years later one of the other St. Joe banks bought us out, and the profit from this formed the basis of whatever investing Walker Jr. did later with the trust that had been set up under his father's will.

Walker Sr. died in April 1959. His parents followed soon after in early summer. In the meantime, Kathie had become pregnant again and, just as in Chicago two years earlier, had to go through the last two months of her pregnancy in uncomfortable heat. One August day as we came back from the doctor's, she began to faint as I walked her into the house. Ann had been born about a week early. Mary obliged her by coming two weeks early, on September 26. My parents had just come through St. Joe with Ray and Doe, on their way back from a vacation in the West, and we had had dinner at our house on the 25th (their wedding anniversary). There were no signs of a baby about to appear that night, so they were surprised when I called them in Chicago the next evening to tell them Mary had been born that morning. The birth was easy this time. Kathie went to the hospital about 8:00 A.M., and by 10:00 A.M. the baby was born. But the nurses were careless, both of Kathie and of Mary. I was left holding Mary for almost an hour, which I thoroughly enjoyed, but the nurses seemed horrified at their negligence when they finally came and found me with her! As for Kathie, the doctor and/or the nurses did not get the placenta out properly, and Kathie bled badly for several days. After almost a week they let her come home, but she was still bleeding. Kathie remembers this whole episode as being what made her a student of Christian Science. Both Kathie and Mary had remarkable healings at that time, which made Kathie see that Christian Science can be relied on. But I also think that she was impressed by the character of some of the Christian Scientists she had gotten to know up to that point.

After three deaths, a wedding (Walker's marriage to Doris Wickham), and one birth in 1959, one might think that life would begin to settle down. And it did. But we realized that St. Joe was not going to be a long-term proposition for us. Whatever I might have thought would be in store for me when I came there in 1958, I could now see the next several years. Instead of trying to work out a *modus vivendi* with my father-in-law (which probably would have been difficult), I was going to run a small financial business that, of itself, had a limited future. Ferd LaBrunerie, my brother-in-law, had come back, just graduated from Harvard in 1958, to run the insurance end of things. There was money to be made in real-estate transactions that could dwarf any possible income from the business itself. But life in this small town on a long-term basis was not for us. I did not feel guilty about wanting to pull out because we both felt we had done much to help Kathie's mother through a horrible period. And I felt that I, as a family member by marriage, had done something to ease the banking dilemma with the government. That, of course, is only my opinion.

With this in our thoughts, we went to Phoenix for a two-week vacation in February 1960. We took Ann along, leaving Mary with Katherine and a sitter. I did not go to Phoenix with the thought of getting a job. If anything, we still were longing for Carmel and often talked of my looking into the banks in California. But in Phoenix we visited some of the people I had worked with at the Northern Trust Bank; in the two years I had been gone, several of the young people there had gone either to Phoenix or California. I went through some interviews at the Valley National Bank in Phoenix and, at the end of our vacation, came back to St. Joe with an offer in hand. Even then I was unsure what to do. But I felt that Kathie's mother was too dependent on us for her social life, in addition to the limited opportunities in St. Joe. Si Rositzky, Walker's closest business associate, tried to dissuade me from moving, pointing out that there were a lot of opportunities in St. Joe that I was not yet aware of. During the month of April we had a series of freak snowstorms coming across from the Colorado Rockies; these probably contributed to our decision, at the end of April, to take the offer. I began work in Phoenix in early June.

To back up slightly: Where had we lived? In St. Joe, after a month or two at the LaBruneries' house, we had moved into a small apartment in Crestview Village. This was a development of ninety-six garden apartments, four units to a building, that Walker had financed at First Federal at a time when he had only $5 million in assets. He had loaned the builder roughly one million and was criticized by the S&L examiners for making too large a loan to one customer. The apartments were needed and quickly filled. The next spring we moved into a new house on a new street that a builder who did his business with First Federal was just developing. It had three bedrooms and, I believe, only a single bath and a single garage. But it was new and needed no work except outside. Our address was 1605 Brookside Drive. We paid $16,500 for the house. When we moved, Katherine was just at the point of selling the family house they had built in 1950, and she bought our house from us.

As for Phoenix, we rented at first at 4502 N. 49th Place in Arcadia (part of Phoenix), just south of Camelback Mountain. We had fifty-five orange and grapefruit trees on the property, and they were irrigated once a week. We were within the Salt River Irrigation District, as was most of old

Phoenix. After a little more than six months, we bought a new, small tract house out in the desert at 3420 Onyx Avenue. When we returned to Phoenix in 2001 for the first time, the tract house was still there, although the neighborhood in general had a messy look to it. The house was just to the north of Squaw Peak, and we have a painting that was done for us in 1965 showing Squaw Peak from our front door. The house on 49th Place had just been torn down and a "trophy" house was being erected in its place. The rest of the neighborhood was still intact.

How does one summarize five years in Phoenix? First of all, HEAT. We were interested in beginning a new phase of our life, but what remains with me from the whole time there is the memory of heat. I had driven out alone, and shortly after I arrived, Kathie flew out with Ann and Mary. It was almost evening in late May when I went to the airport to meet them, but it seemed beastly hot—certainly hotter than I had imagined it would be when we had been there in February. We got a small backyard pool, and I enjoyed sitting in it with the girls every evening when I came home. For three of the five summers we lived there, we did not have an air-conditioned car. So it *is* possible to survive without air conditioning. But I still remember the feeling of being gripped around my middle by a big girdle as I would leave the bank every evening.

The bank had not been sure whether to put me into more training in the Credit Department or make me a loan officer from the start. I prevailed on them (with the vast experience I had had in my two short jobs so far!) to let me start out making commercial loans. They also needed bodies, I think. Many of the commercial loans were personal loans, loans against a person's financial statement, not installment credit. Some of my customers made me feel at home. One, Roger Ernst, had been an Assistant Secretary of Commerce in the Eisenhower Administration, and he had a perpetual loan.

My boss was one of the leading Mormons in Phoenix and spent part of every day on the phone with one of the elders of the church in Salt Lake City. I learned that the bank was honeycombed with Mormons, although the top management were not. The Bimsons, Walter and Carl, had come out from Chicago in the 1930s and built the reputation of the bank. Walter was an art collector and had amassed a large collection of Western paintings.

Phoenix is a good place to raise small children. No clothes to speak of, certainly no winter gear to take on and off five times a day. As the children got a bit older, Kathie heard about a private day school, the Paradise Valley Country Day School. The couple who ran it were Christian Scientists, and the girls went there until we moved to Boston. By that time Ann was in the second grade. We had a summer membership at Mountain Shadows, a winter resort lying between Camelback and Mummy mountains. The water temperature in the large pool got up to the high eighties at times, but it was the coolest thing around. These were the most carefree years of our marriage. We had two small children we enjoyed, Kathie did some work in the Junior League, and we became active in Second Church of Christ, Scientist, Phoenix. When we moved there, it met in a smaller building, probably not meant to be a church. Then we bought land up on Bethany Home Road and managed to get a bank loan for the entire project without any personal guarantees or any pledges from the church members. The church had some older female practitioners who were very active in their healing work, and the friends we made there formed the basis of most of our social life. Brooks Wilder, whom I had known at Harvard, was practicing law in Phoenix. One day at noon, the first week we were in Phoenix, he and I ran into each other on the street. Ridgely Chapline, whom I had known at Wellesley from The Mother Church Sunday School, was Ann's first Sunday School teacher.

I was not making a lot of money, but every year I was given what seemed to me a reasonable increase. I was getting good experience, both in handling credits and in learning how to talk and be comfortable with all sorts of people. I was made an assistant cashier, the first rung on bank ladders, after a year or less, and in another two years I was made an assistant vice president. We were not living in an expensive house, but by 1964 we had begun to look around at something we would want to stay in permanently. The heat bothered me. In fact, every year we began to dread the coming of summer a little earlier. By early May we would have temperatures reaching one hundred in the daytime, although the really bad weather, when it was also humid, was from July through September. In July and August, the thunderheads would gather over the McDowell Mountains to our northeast every afternoon, and whether it rained or not, the humidity was there.

Each fall my parents came for a brief visit. My father loved to take a long car trip sometime after Labor Day, seeing different parts of the West. While we were there, they always came through Phoenix, usually with Ray and Doe. The first year I believe Julia was with them, and we all had Thanksgiving Dinner together at our house. One year my mother came out and stayed for a while with us, and for a while with Pearl Engholm's parents, who had moved to Tempe or Mesa. She thought it might help her arthritis, which had begun to be another major problem for her. We did not do a lot of traveling around the state, as the two girls, and later three, kept us busy at home. We did take a trip to the Grand Canyon once. And in both 1961 and 1962, we took trips to California, which we both still looked at with some envy. We went back to Carmel, which was as good as we remembered, and we also stayed with Roy Alexander and his parents in their house in San Marino.

When we had gotten married, Kathie said she would like to have all her children by the time she was thirty-five. As that time approached, we both agreed it would be great to have one more child. When she found she was pregnant, it looked as if she would not make it by thirty-five. But this one came even earlier than the others—some three weeks. The day before her thirty-fifth birthday, she had a doctor's appointment, and there was no sign of anything happening yet. After supper that evening, she felt a bit queasy, and by 8:00 P.M. I had taken her to the hospital. By 11:00 P.M., Kate had been born, beating the thirty-fifth birthday by one hour. The hospital was crowded, and this time Kathie stayed only over the weekend. I had brought her in on Friday evening, and we came home with Kate Monday morning. Katherine sent out the black woman who worked for her, and we had her excellent help around the house for three weeks.

Besides the visits of my parents, we had gone back to Columbia and Chicago every summer with the girls. We did not have the money for resort-type vacations and, in any case, felt a duty to see our families. We drove every time. I would also go to my annual Christian Science Association meeting in Evanston while we were in Chicago. Ralph had become a lecturer in 1960, so we also saw the Cessnas sometimes when they were in the West. Kathie had become serious in her study of Christian Science and in 1964 flew back to Chicago to have class with Ralph. One of those moments I treasure, and that she may not even remember the same way, was the evening she came back from Chicago. We sat in the living room talking, and I realized that she had glimpsed something of the degree to which Christian Science can transform a whole life. Those moments do not seem to last with any of us long enough, but I felt that her going through class had also bonded us even more firmly together, even though I had never felt that her becoming a Scientist was necessary for us to have a good marriage. Her experience in class, though, undoubtedly made it easier for us to make the next big decision.

We had not been unhappy in Phoenix. I have mentioned the climate. One learns to live with that, even here in New England. The climate probably added to a freer sense of living, although the really good climate of coastal California does that much more. We talked at times of my going over to a bank in California, but there was no event causing me to move on. I did think that I would rather be in investments, in money management, than making loans for years to come. I could see that I would be given more major credits as the years went by, but would probably be just another commercial loan officer for years to come. I did have one credit that was a continual challenge: Nuclear Corporation of America, that later became Nucor and prospered through building small steel mills in small towns where it could get special incentives. We had a term loan with Marine Midland in New York, and twice I had to go to New York to renegotiate the terms of the loan. I remember being in New York with Bob McGee and seeing all the crowds of theater people on the street late at night as we were having a late dinner. Then I came back to Phoenix and walked to my car at the airport. I saw roses blooming and the moon in a clear sky. I looked at the roses and thought, What's so great about roses in December if you aren't doing all the things you should be doing?

We had talked about California as still being a possibility. Then, during the Goldwater campaign in the fall of 1964, we both felt "out of it." Almost all our friends were strong Goldwater supporters, and we could not even talk about politics. At the same time, through an acquaintance in my Christian Science Association, the new editor of *The Christian Science Monitor*, DeWitt John, got in touch with me to ask if I would be interested in coming to Boston to be the paper's business and financial editor. At first, the idea seemed preposterous. I had wanted to work for the paper almost ten years earlier, but my work had gone in another direction, and I had not given the journalism idea any more serious thought. Even Ralph, who I think admired my intelligence, thought it would take a long time for me to fit in to a job like that and did not particularly encourage me to consider it. After some writing back and forth, DeWitt called me one day around Christmas and said, "I think you should come to Boston so we can talk." It was about the time I had to go to New York on business, so I arranged to go to Boston a day or two ahead of that.

* * * *

The upshot of the trip to Boston was that I joined the Monitor. I have placed the asterisks above at this point in the story, because in one sense I have always felt that my "real" adult life began with the move back East. Of course that is not literally true, since I had already had three jobs after the Army years and had grown in some way from each of the experiences. But we moved to Boston in April 1965 and have now lived in the East for over thirty-five years. Most of our experience in raising the girls was here and in Philadelphia, and the high points of my career, whatever one makes of it, were all here in the East. We feel at home in the East, but I think both Kathie and I could feel at home almost anywhere, including Western Europe, except in the South or Texas. Whenever I return to Chicago or to Missouri, it is familiar ground, and the more relaxed manner of life in the Middle West has its own charm. We love the mountainous West, what we know of it. And we both love California, although more the California of 1954 than the thirty-two million people crowding the freeways today. There is a "live and let live" attitude in California that I admire. There is something similar here, although we feel New England, being so conscious of its past, also offers a buffer from too rapid change. And there is the small scale of New England, not only the whole area, but the small scale of each town's independence and sense of its own individual history.

We came back East in early April 1965. We had paid $18,500 for our house in Phoenix in 1961, and my memory is that we sold it for $17,500 a month or two after we had moved. Mary Newman found a rental house in Weston and advised us to take it. There was not much for rent, and we wanted to settle in Weston because we had heard the schools were among the best in the state. We lived at 709 Boston Post Road for the first eight months. Our landlord, Nate Greene, was president of the local bank. I did not know how fortuitous this would be at the time! When we came to finding a house and needing a mortgage that was perhaps more than I could qualify for on my salary, I asked him how I could go about applying for a mortgage. He answered, "You've got it." For the record, we bought a house in February 1966 at 25 Arrowhead Road, which was our home until 1974, for $44,500. We had about $10,000 in stocks at the time (mostly given to us by Kathie's grandmother), and my mother, who had just been widowed, gave us $6,000 to make a total of $16,000. The rest I borrowed. This is all the cash we put into our main house until we came to building on the Cape in 1988. The money for our increasingly expensive homes all came from price inflation, particularly in the housing market. The later homes, while costing more, were more or less in the same category as the Weston house.

I was hired as the Monitor's business and financial editor at a salary of $11,500, or maybe $12,000, but I think it was the lower figure. I had not risen to any high level in Phoenix, where I had been an assistant vice president for two years. I think I was earning $13,000 or maybe a bit more there. Boston was somewhat more expensive, but I do not remember feeling crimped. This was at the end of one of the most quiescent periods as far as inflation goes in recent U.S. history, and that may be one reason the slightly lower salary did not bother me. I was also learning a new trade, as it were, and DeWitt John and I agreed that we were both taking a chance on the other. Ralph Cessna had been concerned that I would have a learning curve regarding newspapering itself—setting up pages, learning how to count in picas, and so on. That was easy, however, and I felt at home with the process within weeks. But I had a lot to learn about writing—one reason I had taken the job, actually! I had to write stories that were usually no longer than seven or eight hundred words: have a lead, tell the story, come to a conclusion, period. I also had to learn a lot about economics. DeWitt had hired me partly because he wanted a business editor from the "outside world"—someone who knew and spoke business and might be able to build an audience of interested business readers, which he felt the Monitor lacked in sufficient number. Whether I ever achieved this I really do not know, but I certainly learned a lot myself! Making commercial loans in a commercial bank had not required an astute knowledge of economics or the business cycle. Now I was forced to write about these things. I had done considerable outside reading in Phoenix, but most of it had been to educate myself on the investment world.

One summer I had spent most of my evenings plowing through Graham & Dodd, the granddaddy textbook on sound investing. That, of course, came in handy. But I had to pick up on all the current economic theories and somehow link this to what I had learned in two economics courses at Harvard. I also had to put out "the page" everyday—that is, edit three or four articles, lay them out on the page with artwork, follow them through the copyediting process, and then proofread the page when it came back from the typesetters. I had two assistants who also wrote, and a secretary. And I had two correspondents in New York who answered to me on the organization chart. In Washington we had three good stringers, who wrote regular copy on economic developments connected with the government. It was more an economics page than a page for business readers who wanted to read about investments, but it had some of both. On the economics, we produced solid copy and were in many respects on par with the material in *The New York Times* or *The Wall Street Journal*. The Monitor was included in meetings to which only a selected group of financial reporters would be invited, such as the International Bankers Conferences held abroad every two years.

The newsroom was less collegial than I had imagined. I quickly felt at home and at ease with several of the correspondents and editors. But by "collegial" I was thinking of a setting in which people traded ideas and had many an informal chat. There was some of this, of course. But I came to see the Monitor as a daily manufacturing operation: By the time we went home each day we had produced a new product. There was a tight schedule, there was no redundant employee, and hence everyone worked at his own job and had little idle time. At times, some of the editors had tried to have a regular group luncheon, but that had apparently not worked for the same reason. Everyone was too busy.

After I had gotten my feet wet, I learned that I was also expected to travel. The first trip that I remember was a World Bank seminar in Washington, at which I got up to speed on the various arms of the World Bank. I wrote four articles, and I remember one of my father's friends, Eldred English, who was a Christian Scientist, telling us later how proud my father was of them. He had been somewhat leery of my taking the job, as up to that time I had already moved around quite a bit, and he also wondered if we had figured out our living expenses, etc.

One reason the move to Boston may be connected in my thought with the change in our lives is that in September

1965 my father died suddenly. He had not been ill, although I now realize that when we visited them in August in Chicago, he had probably been straining his heart. They had been planning a trip to Boston in October, instead of the usual trip out West. He died on a Saturday evening, their wedding anniversary. I flew to Chicago Sunday morning, and the funeral was on Tuesday. My mother held up very well. I realized when it was all over how much my father had come to mean to Ray and Jul. Just before I left for Boston, I called on them in Oak Park. I remember Ray saying, "Well, you have your life to go back to in Boston, with Kathie and the girls. For us, life is over." My father had often stopped in to see them as he was going to or coming from work; during the summer he often brought flowers from the garden. Ray and Jul were a tonic for him, as my mother's paranoia was always something he had to deal with. But I saw then how much he had meant to them—and I suppose having your baby brother die reminds you of your own mortality. My father's passing was hard for me to take. I was not myself for several months. I had not spent much time with him since the summers before I went in to the Army. But there was a close tie between us that may be hard to understand. My mother's chronic problem had probably brought me closer to him. His wonderful letters, two or even three a week (which amazed Kathie), made me feel I was practically with him. We did not talk all that much, that I remember, and he gave me no advice about sex when I was growing up. I had come to appreciate what his life must have been like having the disappointments of the Depression years and then the problems with my mother. And above all, he had never been judgmental. That may be why so many people loved him. At his funeral, the minister said that he had often felt that my father should be up in the pulpit instead of him.

At the Valley Bank in Phoenix, I had traveled very little. I think I had had two trips to New York to renegotiate loans that we shared with a New York bank. Now I had to travel as well as run the page in Boston. After I got into the swing of things, I usually spent a four-day week either in New York or Washington about once a month. I also wrote a weekly financial column, usually on the economy, and did occasional stories in Boston, but most of my other writing came out of the trips. In the course of a year, I would write about fifty columns and perhaps another fifty reportorial pieces.

Then came the pleasure of foreign travel. In 1966 I went on my first foreign trip, a Pan American Airways junket (which the Monitor still accepted) to South America: about two weeks in Venezuela, Brazil (both Rio and Sao Paulo), and Argentina. In 1967 I did my first trip to Europe. This was in a sense a reawakening of the love Kathie and I have for the variety of life in Europe—the different cultures, the history, the scenery, and so on. On this first trip, I believe I went to London, Brussels, Paris, Frankfurt, and Zurich. I was constantly and pleasantly surprised at the reputation the Monitor enjoyed in Europe, entirely apart from any recognition of Christian Science. I often felt I was received for interviews more as a distinguished academician than as a mere journalist. The European trips continued each year and sometimes twice a year: In 1968 I had gone over in the spring, but after the first major currency crisis of the postwar period, I also went over in December.

The Monitor liked to enter the major newspaper contests. I never wrote anything important enough (even in my own eyes!) to be considered for a Pulitzer, but beginning in 1967 my work gained some recognition. That year I received the University of Missouri journalism award for my articles on the U.S. balance of payments dilemma. I went out to Columbia for the award ceremony, held in a motel that Katherine owned a piece of at the time. I think she had been somewhat dubious about my change of career, so this early award probably made things seem better in her eyes. In

1968 I won the Loeb Award, which at least at the time was the most prestigious business-writing award. I received a Loeb honorable mention a year or two later. In 1970 my ten-part series on the U.S. tax system won the John Hancock Award, and in 1973 another long series on the stock market won a second Hancock Award. This was given at a ceremony in Atlanta in the Fall of 1974, after I had gone to work for Girard.

At home the girls continued to grow and thrive. Weston was a wonderful setting in which to raise them. Arrowhead Road had maybe fifty kids on the circular block, so they all had plenty of friends. We did not have a particularly busy social life, as we were busy with work and the kids. But these were very happy years for us all. We did not have the funds to go away on weekends, as some of their friends did. We did not take ski trips. But I do not think the girls felt any deprivation. We lived in a lovely house in one of the best suburbs of Boston. These were the years of the civil-rights marches and then the anti-Vietnam War demonstrations, and I remember Ann telling us one night at the dinner table that we sometimes talked as if revolution was just around the corner. So there was some tumult, but it did not really affect us in our daily lives. I did argue against the war at the paper, but Joe Harrison and Geoffrey Godsell, who ran the editorial pages of the paper, were pro-war. I felt at one point that my job would be in jeopardy if I argued any more with them about it.

The high point of these years (1965-74) was our two trips to Europe as a family, in 1970 and 1971. After each of my foreign reporting trips, I would return with stories about all I had seen and, particularly, eaten. Kathie was unsure that I was not exaggerating about the food. In any case, she wanted to see Europe again, and I thought it would be a great educational experience for the girls and a memorable family vacation. So I took my entire four weeks' vacation and tacked onto that what I called a three-week reporting trip, and we went to Europe for seven weeks. I think my reputation was at its high point about then with DeWitt, or I would not have had the nerve to stretch things out so much. I did do some honest reporting from several countries as well as working on an outside assignment for *Better Homes & Gardens*—some kind of financial advice. I would sit up in bed early in the mornings and work on those articles.

We spent a week in London, staying at the Carlton Tower; then a week in Paris with Elwood and Regina Rickless; then Frankfurt, where we stayed at the house of friends from Weston who were away (they had been transferred to Frankfurt). We then drove to Munich, where some Christian Science people were lending us the key to their house in Malcesine on Lake Garda, Italy—we stayed for an entire week. From there we went back through Munich and Frankfurt, where the Schwarzes, our friends from Army days, lent us their weekend home in Weilburg for another week. Then down through Switzerland, where we visited the Bertschis; on to French Switzerland where we stayed in a small chalet overlooking Lake Geneva; then to Provence, where we met Walker and Doris; and from there back to Paris. At the end of the trip we stayed in a small hotel in Paris near the Whitcombs and they took in the girls. Genevieve prepared most of our meals, and they were delicious. This friendship had flowered, I believe, because I had come to know them both much better in the weeks following Philip's hip operations in Boston in 1969.

I need to say something about friendship and reaching out. This trip was an example of the wonderfully kind things people can do for each other. In this case, often because they are Christian Scientists who feel they have a unique bond, but also friends like the MacFarquhars and Ricklesses, who love to share what they have. We have never been able to adequately repay many of these friends for what they did for us, but I do believe that our own "open house" in Weston, where we entertained so many Monitor visitors as well as others over the years, was the same kind of reaching out, and that "Love *is* reflected in love." This has continued throughout our lives, particularly in regard to transatlantic relations, where a readiness to share so often also helps financially—ourselves as well as those we have welcomed.

We returned from Europe sometime in August, and the day I went back to work, DeWitt was made a Director and John Hughes appointed editor of the paper. This changed everything—one reason 1970 and 1971 were both high points and turning points. John had won a Pulitzer for his reporting on the Indonesian civil war a few years earlier and had been brought back as managing editor. As I now realize was common at the Monitor, either the Directors or the Trustees had some new plan to revitalize it every five years or so. DeWitt had been editor for six years; under him the paper had won three Pulitzers. But because he came from the church side, he had never been cordially received by the veteran staffers, and I suppose the Trustees felt that John could bring a newspaperman's touch to the paper. What he brought was an attempt to copy London journalism: On his desk every day were the flashy London papers. He instilled a new sense of vigor in the newsroom, but he was not a person one could feel close to (unless you were one of his cronies). Our relations were always proper. I had some reputation in the financial writing field by then, and I think he knew he could not touch me. But I was also clearly one of "DeWitt's people," and I soon felt that John's vision of the paper was not one I was comfortable with.

But before continuing with that part of my story, there is one more trip to Europe. After things had settled down in the fall of 1970, the girls still kept talking about our trip and wanted to go again. I was beginning to think about future expenses for college and how I was going to negotiate that, but we all felt we had had the best family experiences so far. Sometime in the spring of 1971, I agreed on another trip, but warned that this would probably be the last one like this. This time we went for only four weeks and were only in France and Switzerland. But it was another great family vacation. This time we visited the Nelsons in a remote town in Provence. Rob had been sent to London by John Hughes and was having a difficult time negotiating his news story with John and Geoffrey Godsell, another Brit, who thought they knew better what was going on. The Nelsons also came to Switzerland and stayed with us at Madame Frank's for a few days. On both trips we also saw Marti and hiked a Swiss mountain with her. In the midst of our visit with the Nelsons in Switzerland, Nixon floated the dollar. Chaos resulted in the financial markets for a few days, and Rob wrote a lovely piece about the Monitor's financial editor being caught napping. I wrote a perceptive piece from Geneva and telexed it immediately, but the new powers in Boston did not understand the importance of what was happening, and the piece ran almost a week later on an inside page.

I am realizing more and more as I write how many people have come and gone in our lives over the years—some are permanent residents, many have made cameo appearances. Others, like the Nelsons, were very important in our lives in the nine years we lived in Weston, but when we came back in 1983, they never had the same place in our lives again. It is impossible, in a family reminiscence, to give all the details, but at least our children will know who we are talking about if they read this history later on. To say that someone drops out of his experience is not a value judgment on that person or on the relationship. It is only a comment on the fact that life continually changes, and we had better be prepared for change until the end. We do have important relationships that have lasted, and that is good—Kathie with Mary Newman, my own with Jack Hoagland, both of ours with Walker. But one also has to accept the fact that, in the kind of society we live in, relationships change for a myriad of reasons, and one had better be prepared for that fact.

In the years I still had at the Monitor I had an interesting variety of trips. In either 1972 or 1973 I went on a junket to planned communities in Europe, something different from my usual financial-capital stops. In December 1972 I went, with the help of AID (Agency for International Development) money, to India for two weeks, first to a development conference in Delhi, then to speak at USIA (United States Information Agency) centers in Delhi, Calcutta, and Bombay. Then, in the late fall of 1973, John Hughes offered me the post of London bureau chief. I do not know to this day if he expected me to take it. Anyhow, I went to London in December 1973 to survey the scene; he jumped to conclusions and put out a bulletin that I had been appointed, etc. This was toward the end of the first oil crisis the West had experienced. Inflation was heating up. In fact, one of the economic events of the early 1970s had been President Nixon's imposition of wage-price controls in 1971. I found that the kind of housing the five of us would need would cost substantially more than I could afford on my Monitor salary—it was then about $20,000—and I also found out that the paper was paying Takashi Oka an extra $10,000 living allowance in Paris. So I came back and presented my case. John said there was no money available, and that according to the cost-of-living figures the Monitor used, there was no need for any adjustment for the London post. So I declined to go. I realized, in turning down the post, especially after he had announced the assignment, that I was probably not going to be his favorite editor. And this in turn led to my being more willing to listen to the siren call from outside.

How we came to live in Philadelphia: This is one of those turning points about which I wonder how logical I have ever been at the moments of change. It was clearly the time to make a change. The girls were growing up, Ann was only a year away from college, and there was no ready money available for college expenses. But they were all getting a good education in the Weston schools, and no one was eager to move. Besides the fact that the college years were looming, inflation for the first time in my working life had become a real issue to deal with. And there seemed to be no prospect of wages at the Monitor approaching what I could earn outside—this plus my frustration with the direction of the paper. But there were numerous jobs in Boston. My work had kept me in touch with the financial community, and the fact that I had some banking background had often helped me gain interviews. Ever since I had spent a summer in Phoenix reading Graham and Dodd, I had said that if I ever went back into banking, it would be on the investment side. And that is how Philadelphia came about. We had become close friends of the Stokeleys. Hugh was an economist at Keystone, and I had occasionally quoted him in articles. He had gone to the Girard Bank in Philadelphia a couple of years earlier to be their economist, and he thought I would be a good Director of Investment Research in their Trust Department. His pressuring me at the right moment (the spring of 1974) led to my going down to be interviewed and subsequently employed.

The move was traumatic. We had all been very happy in Boston. Philadelphia turned out to be inward-looking, and we settled on the Main Line, perhaps the most inward-looking and snobbish part of the city. Kate was unhappy from the start and cried day after day. The day we moved into our house in Wynnewood, Shirley Spelt's husband, David, died. Then Doris LaBrunerie, who had filed for divorce from Walker a few months earlier, came East to try to justify herself to us. The summer was hot and muggy, and we spent weeks stripping wallpaper off this old house and trying to clean it up. Then Nixon left office and the market crashed, creating new challenges at work. As I write about it, I am amazed that we weathered it all so well. It was really just as challenging as the crisis at the Monitor almost fifteen years later. I was forty-five years old and needed to prove myself in what appeared to be a new line of work. I was inwardly confident. I did not know all the latest wrinkles of MPT (modern portfolio theory), which was the trend just then, but I felt I knew the essentials of making investment decisions as well as anyone I worked with. And running the work of fourteen analysts had some similarities to keeping a stable of writers going on business subjects. I had had only three or four full-time correspondents under me, but I had worked with a large number of regular stringers, both in Washington and in Europe.

I sometimes say that I think of the years in Philadelphia as a tour of duty somewhere else, as if I had spent several years in Amsterdam or Basel. That is because at this point in our lives we have lived in Boston since 1965, with the sole exception of the eight and one-half years in Philadelphia. Of course it did not seem like a foreign assignment at the time. We assumed we were going there to stay, or at least not necessarily to return to New England. But even when we were there I did not feel I had put down any roots. Most of my work companions, many of whom were congenial and highly intelligent, lived in scattered areas away from Center City. Our church was only five minutes from the house, but most of the church members were Main-Liners, and moreover, the church was under the influence of a local teacher. So, although we both taught Sunday School at times, we never felt a strong attachment to the church there. Ann and Mary were at Shipley, a private school for girls in Bryn Mawr. We had thought it would be better for them to settle in there in a smaller environment, rather than in the large suburban high school almost around the corner from us. The Shipley education was excellent, but again, the school experience was tainted by the exclusive airs of the Main-Line people. Ann had only one year there and got a special award for her contributions. Mary had three years and managed, but did not love the place. Being captain of the basketball team was probably her main satisfaction. The house we bought was on the edge of the Annenberg estate. It was the best house we had owned, but it had been built in 1937, and nothing much had been done to it since then. But after several years of labor and a few minor improvements, it began to look great. We had paid $44,500 for our house in Weston; it sold in the spring of 1982 for $82,500. We paid $102,000 for the house in Wynnewood, which subsequently sold in 1983 for $230,000. *Sic transit* real estate.

The two most difficult people I worked with at Girard eventually got fired. Hugh was the first to go. After the market drop, he began staying home and playing with his computer. He said that he expected to come in less and less, that his time would be spent doing his economic forecasting, and that that could be done at home. He frequently missed meetings or could not even be reached quickly at his Center City apartment, where he had moved after he left Wilma. I think it was early in 1975 that he was fired. The other person was a man by the name of George Stasen, who had some kind of investment background in Chicago. He was a great talker, and at the time I came, was chairman of the Investment Policy Committee. We got along fine, but I felt we could do just as well without him. When we gave investment seminars for our customers, he and I usually shared the podium, and his style was to prepare a complicated slide show with all sorts of economics and stock market data that probably confused the clients more than anything else. In any case, and much to my surprise, he was also fired late in the fall of 1977, and I was made chairman of the Investment Policy Committee. The Philadelphia banks had an unfortunate habit of comparing the quarterly performance of one of their flagship accounts—the equity pension fund—with their other accounts. During most of Stasen's time, we were at the bottom of the list or close to it (among five major banks). We slowly climbed out of the hole, and by the time I left at the end of 1982, Girard had the best five-year record of the major banks. I do not believe we were first in any of those years, but by consistently being second, we could end up at the top.

These were years of major change in the family. In 1975 Ann went off to Smith College. Two years later Mary entered Principia. We had thought that when Mary left, we would have four years of closer communication with Kate. But we had thought wrong. Kate had her own friends and probably missed very much having at least one sister around. Moreover, she did not like the atmosphere at Shipley (we had entered her there after one year in the public grade school) and wanted to transfer to a prep school in New England. We did not have excess funds and were not sure about the environment in the private schools here at the time, so we said no. In any case, we all got along, but there were some rough spots, as Kate did not always fit in with the Shipley rules. Shipley was also inexplicable in some ways. They fired the female headmistress, but kept her on for a full year after letting people know she had been let go. So the school had little leadership during that time.

I had been earning $21,000 (maybe $22,000) when I left the Monitor. I started at Girard at $35,000, not a high salary in the investment world, but OK for a rather stagnant city such as Philadelphia. By the time I left I had gotten up to $72,000. Moreover, the year we moved, I inherited $35,000 from Doe's estate (she had died in 1972). That was one quarter of the estate, after specific bequests, some of which were relatively large, and decided on by a simple legal formula of leaving equal amounts to each of her siblings or their children. Thus Eunice and I, whose fathers were gone, each got one quarter, and Jul and Ray each got one quarter. That inheritance, coming just then, as well as regular salary increases of some size, changed our financial situation quite nicely. But private-school and college tuitions also took a lot, and we paid for all twelve years of college with our own funds—no scholarships or loans.

I continued to go to Europe at least once a year, this time on an investment trip, but often to some of the same financial centers. Girard had a soft-dollar arrangement with Blythe Eastman Dillon, and I went on several trips with them, hosted by Hugh Eaton, a bon vivant and an entertaining fellow. The trips usually had no more than fifteen people along, so we all got well acquainted. In 1978 I had my first visit to West Berlin, where we spent a few days having talks at the Aspen Institute branch—the same villa, I believe, where the "final decision" regarding the annihilation of the Jews had been made in 1942. In 1979 Kathie went along on the trip with me; it also included a dinner with the Aga Khan in Geneva. After that trip, which was in early spring, we went to London to meet Patricia and Peter Van Pelt, and the four of us drove up to Wales for a long weekend at Port Merion. It was somewhat of a celebration, since 1979 was the twenty-fifth anniversary year for both couples.

To backtrack a bit on trips: For Christmas 1976 Katherine gave us the money to spend two weeks in Jamaica. Jamaica at the time was having considerable unrest, and the State Department advised Americans to be extremely cautious. Fred Spotts called us more than once to see if we were still going to go. We rented a condo from a fellow at Girard. It was in Ocho Rios and was a very pleasant place, with a gorgeous swimming pool plus a sandy beach on the Caribbean. We felt a bit like prisoners there, but we did walk into town once to buy fruit at the local market.

Then, in September 1977, Ann went to Geneva for her junior year abroad. We had friends in Philadelphia whose parents had a large house above Lake Geneva, nearer to Lausanne, and the parents always went to St. Moritz for the holidays. They lent us their house for two weeks, and we all went there to spend the holidays. That was a wonderful time, and the last time, so far at least, that our whole family was in Europe together. Kathie stayed on with Ann for an extra week, and they went to Florence, while I came back on a snowy New Year's day with Mary and Kate to JFK airport in New York. We waited two hours by the curb for Giles Whitcomb to pick us up. The Whitcombs had been in our house in Wynnewood while we were away, and Giles drove up from Philadelphia in a small VW with one window that would not shut. We could barely fit all our luggage and the three of us into the car with him for the ride down to Philadelphia. That same trip was when I was made a senior VP of Girard. I got the call from Frank Bruzda of Girard, while Kathie and I were staying in a hotel for a day or two either in Geneva or Zurich.

From that point on, I was responsible for investment performance at Girard, and as I have already written, it was a very positive period in my career. In January 1980 my mother passed on suddenly. After we had moved to Philadelphia, we had been closer to her retirement home in Pleasant Hill, Tennessee, and we had visited there each spring with the girls, staying at a Tennessee state park nearby. And she had managed, I think every year but her last one, to fly up to Philadelphia to visit us. In the fall of 1979 I had felt I should make a special visit to her. I do not remember now whether I knew something was wrong or not. But since December 1977, when we had been in Geneva, her paranoia had at times resurfaced, and it was always some concern to me that the folks at Pleasant View, the retirement home, would say they could not handle her. But things never got out of control. She was usually calm and sweet and led some of the devotions, so I think they would have put up with much worse behavior. But just after my visit in December, she complained about some kind of swelling or internal growth. Whether they paid enough attention to her complaints, I do not know. But one night I came home from work, and Kathie said they had called to say that something was wrong, but nothing that I need come down for. At five the next morning they called from the local hospital to say she had died.

My mother's passing removed a financial concern. When my father died, she had about $50,000 to invest, including the sale of her house. I had not managed the money particularly well. I put most of it in two mutual growth funds, but the 1970s had not been good market years. I had also made one or two more risky investments that did not turn out well, and she had given us $6,000 for our house in Weston. I had to make up whatever deficiency she had in her bills each month after she spent her social security and my father's small pension, and by the time she died there was very little left. The late 1970s saw severe inflation also, so her retirement-home costs had escalated each year.

In the summers of 1980 and 1981, we decided to go back up to New England. In 1980 we rented a house on Lonnie's Pond in Orleans for the month of August, and we decided to buy a lot there. It was another one of those important decisions that was made without much hesitation, but it had a lot of background. We missed New England. It is the only place I know in America that has a small enough scale to feel homey. We were both used to it, and this is where we had met, etc. Moreover, the climate in Philadelphia was awful. The Mid-Atlantic is similar to Missouri. Someone had told me that Philadelphia would be just like Boston. In no way was it like Boston, climate being only one aspect. So somewhere I had gotten the idea that, once Kate was out of college (presumably 1985), we would think of a way to retire early to the Cape and that I might even set up my own investment business there. In the third week of August, I went back to Philadelphia for a week's work, and Kathie went out with local brokers looking at lots for sale. When I came back, we looked at five or six she had located and liked that we could also afford, and without much hesitation, we agreed on what came to be our home at 15 Hayward Lane. We paid $45,000 for the lot. The woman who was developing the entire street took back a mortgage, which we paid off in three or four years.

The winter of 1980-81 was unusually hectic. In January I went on an investment trip with Hugh Eaton *et al.* to Japan, Hong Kong, Singapore, and Australia. Almost as soon as I returned, I went to Florida to meet Kathie, who had just returned from a Caribbean cruise with her mother. Then, either then or a month later, we were at Kiawah in South Carolina with some of the girls for a brief vacation. Meanwhile, Kate was in her senior year at Shipley. She was dissatisfied with it and, according to Kathie, had done nothing toward applying to colleges while I had been away. One day, when Kathie was either in Florida or out in Missouri with her mother, I had a call from Shipley saying Kate was missing. I took a train out to Wynnewood, ran to our house, were she was not to be found, then called Shipley again, and they said they had found her sleeping in someone's dorm room.

In March Kate went up to New York for three weeks to intern in Judge Thomas Griesa's law office. She deserves a lot of credit for arranging the internship, which Shipley only grudgingly approved. In any case, in looking back later, I realized that there had been about three months of hyperactivity and a lot of strain. On a Monday morning in March, I realized something was wrong with me. But Kathie drove me to the station, and I went to work anyhow. I apparently was having a heart attack, although some ignorance on my part probably prevented me from realizing what was happening. The next few days were memorable, and I will not recount them here. The Christian Science practitioner who worked with me was absolutely wonderful. I stayed home for a week, telling the office I had the flu, and managed to go back to work the next Monday. It was some months before I could climb the stairs comfortably, and I was careful about my trips to New York. And it was summer before I tested myself in any serious way: We came back to the Cape in August, and I found I could swim without hesitation.

This incident was important, not only for the healing I had, but because it had a lot to do with my willingness to return to the Monitor two years later. A couple of other incidents also made their contribution. In the summer of either 1981 or 1982 I had to represent the bank at the dedication of a new medical clinic in north central Pennsylvania. I was terribly impressed with the dedication of the doctors there and even wrote a memo to myself at the time more or less challenging myself to some similar dedication. Then John Franklin died, of some sudden, cancer-like illness, in the summer of 1982. And Geoffrey Godsell, who had been no particular friend of mine in Boston, but had dedicated his life to making a major contribution at the Monitor, died. These reminders of how short life can be made me think of the relative importance of what I was doing and surely softened me up when the approach came in the fall of 1982 to come back to Boston.

Two other items about Philadelphia first: the General Accident Insurance Company and the Barnes Foundation. After I became chairman of the Investment Policy Committee at the bank, I was put on the Board of the Barnes and made a member of the investment committee of the General Accident Insurance Company, the U.S. subsidiary of the Scottish General Accident. I enjoyed participating in making the broad investment decisions at the General Accident, and felt in some ways as if that was more of an individual contribution than what I did as head of the Investment Policy Committee at Girard. I was accepted as an equal, and my views were seriously considered, as they were at Girard, but something about the mix of the other people at the General Accident gave me the confidence that I could start my own investment firm up on Cape Cod if I started when I was young enough.

As for the Barnes, that was a combination of comedy and tragedy. Girard named the Treasurer of the Barnes, under the doctor's indenture. And the Treasurer was one of five Trustees of the Barnes. The others were still largely holdovers from Barnes's day, although he had died in an automobile collision in 1951. Sid was the Chairman. He was a lawyer, and his father had been Barnes's lawyer. Sid was afraid to make any decision that met with opposition from Miss DeMazia, a Belgian woman who had allegedly been Barnes's mistress. And DeMazia wanted no changes at all. The Barnes endowment, at $7 million, was insufficient to carry on the work of the foundation far into the future, and the bylaws prevented it from investing in anything but government bonds. But I enjoyed the business meetings, sitting among the famous paintings. My sole accomplishment in the five years I was there was to get the board to agree to institute a small fee for the art course that DeMazia taught, about the same per lecture as one paid for a movie at the time. DeMazia abstained from the vote.

My family and I had spent the month of August in Orleans in both 1980 and 1981, at the same house on Lonnie's Pond. In 1982 we had not made up our minds about a vacation when Joe and Marzee Harrison asked if we would like to stay in their house in Orleans during October, when they would be at their chalet in Switzerland. We knew that autumn is good on the Cape and accepted their offer. I do not remember what other traveling we may have done during the summer. When we arrived at the Cape in October, I got a call from Jack Hoagland, asking me to have lunch with Earl Foell, the Monitor's editor, the following week, and "to listen to what he had to say."

What transpired was an offer, entirely unexpected, to return to the Monitor as its managing editor. The following Saturday, Tony Periton, the then Manager (whom Jack was about to replace) asked if he could come to the Cape to visit. The purpose of that trip was to coax me to say yes. Kathie and I had ample time during the course of the month to decide what to do. I had often said I was still interested in journalism, but not in a daily paper. The kind of journalism I liked was more thoughtful, and although I recognized the importance of daily news, I felt that the Monitor in particular had a more important mission. Jack was about to come onto the scene as Manager, and I knew I would look forward to working with him. Moreover, in September the Mellon Bank had agreed to acquire Girard, and if the deal went through, my position could have been in jeopardy or, even worse in my eyes, we might have been asked to move to Pittsburgh. In the end, I decided to make one more move, still thinking in the back of my mind that this might get us to Orleans even sooner and even to launching my own money-management firm. So in November we put our house on the market, and I began work in Boston the day after New Year's, 1983. Kathie did not enjoy leaving our house in Wynnewood, which was the most elegant of any of the homes we had. We had also done a lot of the work on it ourselves and had lived there as long as we had lived in the Weston house.

As I look back on it almost twenty years later, this decision may have been the most important career decision I made. Not for what I did at the Monitor, but the fact that the two books I have written, my own development in the areas of Christian Science and spirituality, and my interest in the formation of Christianity would probably not have occurred had we kept on as we were in Philadelphia. I was delighted to be back in New England, and it shortly seemed as if I had never left. But from the start there was turbulence, and in fact, almost the entire ten-plus years I was to be at the Monitor this time around were years of turbulence.

Not long after I came back, Jack intimated that I would probably succeed Earl as editor shortly. I did not take his remark as a definite commitment, and that was fortunate, for within five months the Directors had decided to make Kay Fanning the editor. This came as a shock to both Earl and me, but more for Earl, as he had had no inkling that he was about to be tossed aside. Kathie and I made a trip to Alaska to spend a weekend with Kay after I had first met her in Boston. Kay settled in during the fall of 1983, and when she married Amos (Mo) Matthews in January 1984, Kathie and I gave the wedding dinner for them at our house in Lincoln. We worked together satisfactorily, but I did not feel she had much of a sense of what the Monitor was, and on at least one occasion she told me she had not felt competent to take the job.

Sometime during the spring or early summer of 1984, I had the idea of running a Monitor contest. I do not know how this started, and it was certainly not typical Monitor procedure. But I presented it to Kay and the other editors, and they let me pursue it. The idea was to have an essay contest, called Peace 2010, in which the writers would give their version of how peace came to the world in the ensuing twenty-five years. The essays could be fairly lengthy, with the contest ending at the end of 1984. But before getting to that, the contest idea apparently struck a chord with the Christian Science Board of Directors, and when I came back from a short vacation in August, Harvey Wood told me that the idea had blossomed into something for the whole world. The Church had decided to put on a video conference that would be downlinked to Christian Science churches worldwide. The conference would take place in Boston and London, and I was asked to host the presentation in London. The meeting was eventually set for December 8, and much of that autumn was spent in working out the concept for and the details of the program. Kathie and I went to London at the start of December and rehearsed that entire week with the panel I was to chair, comprising David Willis, David Winder, Bev Pond, and Charlotte Saikowski. The evening of December 8 we broadcast, or televised, our segment from the observatory at Greenwich, literally straddling the line between the eastern and western hemispheres. We had a small TV audience, maybe fifty people. Kathie and I had managed to invite the Van Pelts as our guests; most of the people were prominent Christian Scientists from the London area. Our segment talked about covering the major trends underlying the news from the areas of the world the various correspondents worked in. The major follow-through from the program came when I got back to Boston. Harvey Wood said that he felt as if he belonged to a wholly new church, and from that moment onward, I think the Directors made their decision to take the Monitor worldwide through the development of TV. It was about this time that Kay Fanning began to have her disagreements with the Board, as she felt the ground shifting from under the only territory with which she was familiar—a daily newspaper.

Before going on, I need to mention how we settled back in Boston. We wanted to stay in the western suburbs and started looking in Weston. We also looked in Wellesley, Lincoln, and Concord. We found Wellesley too "suburban." We were most familiar with Weston, and of course it was the most convenient for running back and forth to Boston. But we also had a limited number of houses in our price range to look at and wondered if we would want to settle down exactly as we had lived ten years earlier. We finally found a very modern house, with unfinished vertical redwood siding, on three levels, in Lincoln. Its only drawback was that it backed onto the railroad track. At about the same time, we finally sold our house in Wynnewood for $230,000 and bought this one for $235,000. For the record,

I had just had a raise at Girard to $72,000 and came back to the Monitor for $62,000—again taking a pay cut. But that was ample to live on. We were only two years away from Kate's presumably finishing at Stanford, and in any case, I did not really assume in 1983 that I would be staying at the Monitor as long as I did. The Lincoln house was not as elegant as the Wynnewood house, but it was an exciting house to live in for the ten years we owned it. It also had a swimming pool, and we did a lot of entertaining outdoors, including several Monitor parties. Over the postwar decades, Lincoln has been a leader in conservation and also in trying to maintain some mix of affordable housing. It has abundant conservation and marshland, and we were glad that we had finally settled there instead of in Weston. But the whole area made us feel like we had come home, another reason it was hard to leave it even after we had intended to retire to the Cape.

The Directors were intent on moving the church and the Monitor forward into a new information age. During these years they began to experiment with radio in a big way and to edge into television. The next big TV event was in 1986, when we put on another downlinked show, this time for journalism students at various colleges. The show was too complicated and overproduced, but it made 1986 a banner year for travel. Just after New Year's, Brooks Whitfield, Netty Douglass, and I went to Vienna to scout out a venue for the segment to be produced there. Eventually we got to use part of Schoenbrunn Palace. Also in January we went to Brazil to look for a site there, and we eventually got permission to use the Foreign Ministry building in Brazilia (although that segment of the show was canceled). We also went to Japan to look for a site there, and to England for the same purpose. We went to Chartwell, thinking we might use Churchill's own home for the venue. The house was closed, at least during the winter, but we toured it and decided it was not the right location. Eventually Ditchley Park was chosen as the location, and Kathie and I went over in April to prepare for the event. This was just a few days after President Reagan had bombed Libya, and it was not a particularly easy time to be taking a trip. Our panel at Ditchley Park was to discuss Third World issues and terrorism, and most of the questions that came in from the students had to do with terrorism. There were many prominent Christian Scientists from England and the Continent staying as guests at the house that weekend. After the show Kathie and I went to Switzerland to visit the Bertschis in Zurich and in Klosters for a few days. I think I was in England three or four times during 1986, and toward the end of the year I had to go to Japan once more. It was when I returned from Japan on an early December night that Kathie met me at Logan and told me in tears that Katherine was probably in her last weeks. Kathie went out to Kansas City two or three times during the month, and her mother passed on the morning of New Year's Day, 1987.

To backtrack: In 1985 Ann and Ed decided to marry. They had been living with each other since 1980 in Washington. They came up to Lincoln for the wedding, which was at First Parish. We had two dinners at the house and the wedding reception at the Pierce House in Lincoln. Shortly after their wedding, we went off with DeWitt and Morley John on a vacation to Spain and Portugal. Morley had made most of the reservations in Madrid, Toledo, Granada, Seville, and Cordova in Spain. We then went to Evora in Portugal. It was at the end of this trip, in Evora, that DeWitt had an apparent heart attack and died that night in his sleep.

In the fall of 1985 we began to do a monthly half-hour TV program. It was produced in New York in a studio on 42nd Street. I went down for several of the first shows. My work was gradually evolving into planning the TV operation, along with Jack and Netty, and at the end of 1985 I gave up my managing editor title at the Monitor. I had various titles for the next three years and do not even remember what they all were or how one succeeded another. It was a very fluid period! About a year later, we began to produce the same show up in Boston, using the WGBH studio in Allston. We went from the monthly pilot show to a weekly. The main challenge was getting carriage at decent times, and this in turn led to the decision to have our own TV channel and to purchase Channel 68 in Boston.

In the autumn of 1987, Jack presented a plan to end the deficit of the newspaper to the Trustees of the Christian Science Publishing Society. It was all tied in to a planned ramping up of the TV effort. Kay was given the assignment, and a considerable budget, to spend up to twelve months preparing a business plan to fulfill the goals the Trustees had adopted. Two major things happened during the following twelve months that changed my life. The first had nothing to do with the paper or TV. The Directors of the Church held a retreat (I was not a part of it) for several days that same autumn and came back from it asking me to leave the paper and everything else I was doing to write a history of the Christian Science movement and a one-volume biography of Mrs. Eddy. I was to be given five years to complete the project and would have the same salary considerations I would have had if I had stayed with the Monitor. This represented a huge undertaking for me. I had often expressed the desire to explore more of how the ideas of Christian Science came to Mrs. Eddy. Just a few months earlier, Jack and Netty and I had been in Japan together, and on the way back we had stopped overnight at the church's new shortwave station in the Marianas. I remember floating in the surf on the beach there and then talking over some of these ideas with Jack and Netty. Now I had the opportunity to search the church archives, without any restrictions. I set to work on the biography first, because I felt in some ways it would be an easier project than trying to write the history of the movement. So, for the next six to eight months, I immersed myself in the archives, mainly reading Mrs. Eddy's own correspondence.

The second thing that occurred was that, by summer 1988, it was clear that Kay was not going to come up with a plan to substantially reduce the paper's deficit. Jack then asked me to step aside for a while from the writing project and work on a plan for the paper. This I did with the help of two outside consultants. We came up with a smaller paper, but smaller mainly because it contained no more small ads. The news hole was shrunk only slightly. The editorial staff had grown to about 175, and I believe my plan envisaged a staff of just over one hundred. The Trustees met on October 31 to hear Kay's report and to review the plan I had drawn up. Kay's report, which included the recommendation that she be able to bypass the management and in effect be the publisher, was greeted with silence. In the days that followed, the tension grew. The plan we had worked on internally was leaked to *The Boston Globe* as "the Nenneman plan." Finally, over the Veterans Day weekend, matters came to a head. Harvey Wood was unable to reach Kay by phone. On the next Monday, Kay and two other editors resigned in protest, apparently expecting to create a rift among the Directors that would lead to their being recalled. In haste, I was given the choice of being editor or editor in chief. I was not really that interested at this point in running the paper and hoped to get on with the biography I had now begun. So Dick Cattani, who had been chief editorial writer for five years and on whose intelligence, integrity, and loyalty I could depend, was made editor, and I took the supernumerary title, one that had been used only twice before and each time for a unique situation.

The weeks after mid-November were critical ones. We did not know how much of the Monitor staff would walk out. Actually, none did, but morale was badly shaken by the negative spin that Kay and the departing editors had put on events. The Directors called a special meeting of all the Christian Science teachers on short notice—the week before Thanksgiving—at which Jack and I both presented major talks defending the steps the paper was taking, yet trying not to criticize the people who had left or harm their reputations. Then, early in December, Kathie and I went on a short trip to Europe, which we had planned months before, mainly to Germany, where we enjoyed the Christmas fair in Frankfurt and the Bach Christmas Oratorio in the rebuilt Opera House just a few blocks from our first apartment in Frankfurt back in 1955. Then we went to Baden Baden to visit Dieter and Christa Forster, who were on vacation there. I also made a quick plane trip to Hamburg to visit a printing plant doing color printing, and we ended up with a few days in London, coming home just a few days before the bombing of Pan Am Flight 103 over Lockerbie, Scotland—another event that tended to mar the freedom of travel for some time. By the time I returned to Boston the decision had been made to print the Monitor in color, and in stealth the plans had been made to have new printing plants ready to go by January 1. Of necessity, the old printers were not told of our plans until the day before, and this caused a good deal of criticism (they were recompensed, though, for the interruption of business we caused). In January we began the layoffs, cutting the staff to roughly the number I had suggested. The layoff package was generous, and my memory is that about two-thirds of those we needed to lay off took the voluntary package. At the same time, Dick Cattani partially succumbed to the turmoil and was at home for several weeks. So that entire winter I spent largely in the newsroom working on whatever problems emerged from day to day.

By the summer of 1989 I had some time again to work on the biography. But by now I had had another idea—perhaps coming out of the blue as had the peace contest in 1984—that what the Christian Science movement needed even more was a book positioning Christian Science in human thought, its relation to Christianity in a broader sense, its relation to modern thought about the physical universe, and so on. I took this idea to the Directors, and they told me to go to work on it. So for the next year or so I worked on this book. George Spitzer, who became of even greater use to me (as well as a good friend) when it came to getting the biography published, was consulting for the Trustees at the time and had substantial connections in the publishing industry from his twelve years with Book-of-the-Month Club. He took my manuscript to HarperCollins, and they agreed to publish what came to be *The New Birth of Christianity*. The book appeared in early 1992, but it had essentially been written a year prior to its publication.

One bonus from returning to the Monitor was an invitation from the German government in 1991 to be the guest of Chancellor Kohl, with other newspaper editors, on a VIP tour of the new Germany. After the fall of the Berlin Wall in 1989, one of the most emotional moments of my entire life, I wanted to see how the country would come together again. I went over as a journalist in March 1990 when they had the first elections in the East and had my first look at East Berlin. I also went to Leipzig and Dresden to see them in their then dreary states. Later that year the Church held a youth conference in Hamburg, and I was asked to give one of the talks in German. Kathie and I went over for that at the end of September. As it happened, the conference ended just a day or two before October 3, the date that had been set for reunification. So we went on to Berlin as the guests of Joachim Trapp. The night before the reunification we had dinner with the Trapps in Potsdam at the villa (the Cecilienhof) where Truman, Churchill, and Stalin had met at the end of the war. Then we marched with two million others and stood in front of the Reichstag as the reunification hour approached. And the next day we actually drove through East Berlin in Achim's big BMW. So the trip in September 1991 was not my first to the East, but it was for

Kathie. Of all the Monitor travel I ever did, that trip, of course, takes the cake. We dined with the Kohls at their house in Bonn. We flew in Erich Honekker's old plane from Bonn to Leipzig. We were chauffeured around in black Mercedes—one for each couple—even from the tarmac at Berlin's Tegel airport, from which we went straight to the Schloss Bellevue for luncheon with President von Weizsacker. (Upon being introduced, he said something very kind about Christian Science to me, but it was almost *sotto voce*, and it was not the occasion to ask, "What did you say?")

As my book was about to come out in early 1992, all hell broke loose at the TV end of the Monitor. Since November 1988, when I had become editor in chief, we had had a nightly TV show, first with John Hart as anchor and then John Palmer. The TV operation, including the 24-hour Channel 68 with many different programs, was draining money out of the Church at too fast a rate, and when the dissidents succeeded in blocking the funds the Church had expected to receive from the Bliss Knapp estate after his book was published, the operation had to either fold, be sold, or be drastically reduced. After several days of attack from *The Boston Globe*, with one-sided information obtained from the dissidents, Jack and Netty resigned, Harvey Wood resigned as a Director, and a new management took over. By this time I had just about finished the manuscript of my biography, but I was also involved in editing several of the older biographies to correct mistakes in them and to add new introductions. I was offered a chance to become the archivist of the Church, which did not interest me at the time, or to retire under the same layoff package being offered the TV people. I had expected that, after the biography was finished, I would be able to return to the Monitor as some kind of contributing columnist and figured that I had something to offer the paper, if only the experience of being over sixty. But the Church finances were very tight at the moment, and perhaps I was judged as being part of the Hoagland and Wood crowd. At any rate, amidst all the turmoil going on in 1992, I had already told Kathie that my goal was to get away within another year. So I could hardly complain if the organization took its own steps that so closely coincided with my desires at that moment. In any case, they wanted me to finish up some work on the other biographies that were being rereleased as part of the Twentieth Century Biographers Series. I said that this could probably be wound up within a period of months. In fact, I believe I was kept on the payroll at full salary until May 1993, although I did some of my work at home. By the way, I had come back in 1983 at a salary of $62,000; for the last four or five years there, though, I was earning $120,000, a salary roughly comparable to that of a Congressman or Federal judge at that time. Not a corporate salary, but also not too bad for a nonprofit organization and one in whose goals I deeply believed.

During the last two years there, I did manage to make two additional trips to Germany. A group there, funded by the federal government, put on two seminars in the spring of 1992 and 1993, both in Berlin, called Forum fuer Deutschland, to which they invited me. The meetings included many participants from the eastern bloc countries and appeared to me to be a German attempt to establish some footings with their neighbors to the east as well as to engage them in the kind of freewheeling discussions we are accustomed to in the West.

So the move back to Boston in 1983 had lasted some ten plus years, much longer than I had anticipated, but also ending more abruptly than I expected. Sometime before all these events at the Monitor transpired, we had turned our thoughts to the Cape and our possible retirement there.

The first few years back in Boston, we had been so preoccupied with work and getting resettled that we had not even visited the Cape. Sometime in 1984 we went down to Orleans and found that a house with a Hawaiian-style roof had been built across the street from us on what we had thought would be only wooded land. Kathie was so upset that she wanted to sell our lot. But as time went on she got used to the house, and today it seems well settled into our street. After Katherine died in 1987, Kathie got a modest inheritance from her as well as one-third of the money from her grandparents' trusts. Moreover, in 1981 we had sold the small shopping center in Columbia, in which we owned a partial interest. We had taken back a large mortgage, payable in full in November 1988. Assuming that the mortgage would get paid when it fell due, we could anticipate that we would have enough money to carry two houses for awhile, until my retirement. During the spring and summer of 1987, we engaged an architect in Orleans and made weekly trips down to the Cape to discuss our plans with him. Late that fall he came up with a drawing that was more or less complete, and with his encouragement, we put the plans out for bid. We had not actually expected to build that soon. The bids, at just over $300,000, came in somewhat lower than I had expected, and I went to a local bank to see how much they would lend us. Since we already owned the land outright, and its value had escalated during the 80s, and because the bank wanted to keep the construction business going, they said they would lend us the entire contract amount. Construction started early in March 1988, and we continued to go to the Cape weekly to check on its progress. The house was finished in late November, and we did get paid off on the mortgage when it fell due. This was not enough to pay for the new house, but it reduced the new mortgage to an amount that we could comfortably carry as long as I was working.

That fall Ann and Ed moved up to Boston; they moved in with us for what eventually was a full year, so it was convenient to have the second house to go to on the weekends.

They shipped their furniture to Orleans, and for the first year the living room was piled high with their boxes. In 1989 Mary and Vic decided to get married, and they had their wedding ceremony in the house in Orleans in late October. Ann and Ed bought their condo in late 1989, and the house in Orleans remained only partially furnished until we sold the Lincoln house in the fall of 1993 and moved to Orleans.

The last family event to take place while we lived in Lincoln was Kate and Will's wedding, in August 1993. We held the rehearsal dinner and reception at The Country Club in Brookline, and they were married by Judy Hoehler at First Parish in Weston. We sold the house in Lincoln for $480,000, a measure of what had happened to real estate prices during the ten years we had owned it. So, by the fall of 1993, all of our children were married, and we had come to Orleans to begin a new chapter in our lives.

Retirement from paid employment was not a shock, but the new life took a few years to get used to. I had often said I envied Kathie's brothers for being on their own, and I do not think I would have done the few things I have done since 1993 if I had worked much longer. It does take time to learn to adjust to a schedule one makes for oneself, and I am still learning that one does not settle things once and for all just because one has retired.

After we had sold the house in Lincoln, we fully expected to make the Cape our only home and stay here (where I am writing this) for the rest of our lives. That was in the fall of 1993. After a year and a half there, it seemed obvious to me that we would never completely leave Boston, at least not as long as all three girls live there. But in addition to that, there were all the associations, both with persons and institutions, that we had cultivated over half a lifetime, if one does not count the Philadelphia years. I was still chairman of the Boston Committee on Foreign Relations, although I gave up that role shortly after moving. I was a member of the Boston Economic Club. We had our church associations, both with The Mother Church and in Weston. I was just completing my first term of three years as a member of the Harvard Graduate Council. And so on. So, in the summer of 1995, we bought a small condominium in Lincoln and moved the furniture we had put in storage into that in late summer. It was wonderful to have a home to go to in Boston again! During the preceding almost two years, we had had hardly a single week when we had not been up in Boston, and it was not convenient to stay with any of the children. Once we had stayed in a Marriott Hotel, and that seemed even more ridiculous and certainly did not feel like a home. So, since 1995, we have commuted to Boston weekly, just as we commuted to the Cape from 1988 until 1993, only the commute is in the other direction now, that is, we do spend more time here than in Boston.

When I had left the Monitor, the final scene had not yet been played out with my biography of Mrs. Eddy. I was largely satisfied with the manuscript, although the last chapter, into which I had plugged a lot of miscellaneous quotes from her letters that seemed too pungent or important to be omitted, had not pleased all of the Directors (who had read the manuscript). I decided to omit this chapter and, instead, to write an epilogue touching on issues that might affect the position of Mrs. Eddy and her discovery in the future. However, even before this change, the Directors had authorized George Spitzer to seek out a publisher and to place an order for 25,000 copies, so I know the book as a whole met with their approval. (At the time I had been given the assignment, I had been told, in effect, to write it as I saw it— there were to be no strings attached. It was clear, though, that I had been asked to write about her partly because I had been a student of her teachings for almost fifty years.)

In 1993 the Church was still strapped for funds. Interest in the book fell by the wayside, and the publishers George approached said, in effect, that this sounded like a "church book." Then, in 1994, two new Directors were brought in, and the project seemed to slide even further. Finally, sometime in 1995 I asked if they would have Archives check my hundreds of quotes for accuracy and then give me permission to use them. This process took the better part of a year, I would say going from the spring of 1995 well into 1996. Finally, in the spring of 1996, after one of the Directors had said he would assign one of their own editors to go over the manuscript with me and then delayed the start of that, this same Director wrote to me giving me permission to proceed with the book in any way I wanted. At this point, George offered to publish it himself under his Nebbadoon Press imprint, which he had already used for a few other books. During the summer and fall of 1997, Kathie and Jane Spitzer and I worked diligently editing the manuscript. I wrote quickly, and besides many questions of fact they wanted me to check up on, there were stylistic matters that would have embarrassed me if their careful editing had not caught them. In November 1997 the book *Persistent Pilgrim: A Biography of Mary Baker Eddy* appeared, probably to the surprise of the Directors. I wrote them thanking them for permission to go ahead with the book, but never even had an acknowledgment of my letter. At first the Monitor did not want to advertise the book, but that hurdle was overcome. The orders trickled in, and by the summer of 1998 about three thousand of the first printing of five thousand had been sold. Then what appeared to be a case of serendipity occurred. A vicious book attacking Christian Science was published, and the husband of the author had good publishing connections in New York. The book got more attention than it deserved. One Friday night I had a call here on the Cape from the Directors, asking me if I could read the book over the weekend and respond with an internal memo. The book was delivered by FedEx Saturday morning, I read it quickly and wrote a few memos, and I had a letter from the Directors expressing their thanks to someone they could trust so thoroughly. I felt that somehow a logjam with my own book might have been broken, so I sent one of them a sampling of some of the mail I had been receiving from readers of the book. Within two weeks, maybe less, I had a call from the Chairman of the Board asking if they could "have the book" immediately.

It has still never had a Monitor review, but the book has now had four printings. I have written about this in more detail than I intended, but the entire episode was a piece of unfinished business for me when I left in 1993, and although I was delighted to get it published in late 1997, the story really ends with the Church wanting to have it for sale and distribution in late 2000.

During this same period, I did extensive reading on the early Christian church, on the Bible, and on alternative healing—subjects that have more commonality for a Christian Scientist than they might for someone else. In 1999 and 2000 I had the opportunity to give a paper on the development of the Jesus story in the New Testament and another one on alternative healing, as well as papers on various periods in the life of Mrs. Eddy. In 2000 I also was asked to speak on two occasions at Principia College. I do not see myself doing a lot of public speaking, but I want to continue my reading—and possibly writing—on the subjects that seem the most vital to me.

The President of David L. Babson & Co., whom I knew only slightly from the Committee on Foreign Relations, called me in 1994 and asked if I would go on the board as an independent trustee of a new group of mutual funds they were establishing. I was glad to have an additional motive for keeping current on the economy and agreed to do this, and I was, until recently, one of the independent trustees of the

DLB Funds. I have also done some community service work, of varying degrees of value. In 1993 or 1994 I joined the Executive Service Corps of New England, and I have done six or seven projects for them. The two with the best outcomes were both long-range strategic plans for the Nauset Regional School system here on the Cape and for the Latham School, also on the Cape, a residential school for disturbed teenage girls. For three years I was on the Orleans Finance Committee and was chairman two of those years. After that exercise was over, I went on the Board of our condo in Lincoln, also for three years. There are ample opportunities for community service work when one is free of a regular job. The main challenges are to choose wisely, to not become overly involved out of a sense of needing to be wanted, and to do the things that in some way contribute to one's own growth. I had also told Kathie that when I retired we could do some of the things we had put off while I had no time for planning long vacations. And that brings me to the most pleasant part of these years—travel.

My last trip for the Monitor was to attend the Forum fuer Deutschland in the spring of 1993. As soon as I was completely free, we went back to Europe that fall to Germany, Austria, and Switzerland. In the early spring of 1994, we did an Elderhostel opera trip to Berlin. Later that year we did a Harvard barge trip on the Rhine, Main, and Danube, starting in Cologne, going up the Main past Frankfurt, then over the new high canal linking the Main and the Danube, and down the Danube to Vienna. In 1995 and again in 1998, we did a major trip to Scandinavia. Both times we visited with our friends Hanne and David Lansing, who have a summer house on the Gold Coast north of Copenhagen. In 1998 we all did the two-week boat trip up around the North Cape as far as the Russian border.

In 1996 we did a Harvard trip to Istanbul, the Greek islands, and western Turkey. It included a week of sailing on the *Sea*

Cloud, surely the best trip we could ever imagine. Two of the days we had high winds and went under full sail—all thirty-eight sails! In 1997 we did a spring trip to France on our own, and later that spring did a Harvard trip to Malta, Sicily, the Aeolian Islands, and the Amalfi peninsula. In the fall of 1998 we did a Yale trip with the Wreans to New Mexico. The trip was led by a former Yale president, Howard Lamar. In 1999 we did another Sicily trip, this time with Smith College; this one included several places in Sicily we had not yet seen as well as a few days in Rome at the end. In 2000 we again went to France on our own in the early spring; we stayed mostly in Provence, but had four days in Paris at the end. And in the fall of 2000 we did a Smith trip to Spain with Mary Newman and Bill and Wendy Wrean. This was followed by our own traveling in Alsace and southern Germany, including the Passion Play in Oberammergau, which Kathie and Mary Newman had seen fifty years earlier. In 2001 our "vacation" was a month's intensive schooling in French in Villefranche on the Cote d'Azur.

I went to California in 1999 and 2000 to give talks on Mary Baker Eddy at Frank Darling's seminars. We also spent time in Carmel, San Luis Obispo, and Santa Barbara. Also during those years we were in the Tampa area in Florida for the same purpose. We flew to Phoenix in 2002, the first time we had been there since we left in 1965. We visited Morley John and saw our former home. The desert area was greatly built up, compared to thirty-five years earlier. Kathie and I also attended a week's conference at Chautauqua, New York, where we heard Karen Armstrong speak. She writes on religions of the world and I admire her greatly. We also attended the Shaw Festival, in Niagara-on-the-Lake, every summer from 2000 through 2006. It is a week-long session of plays by Bernard Shaw and his contemporaries. I gave an inspirational talk in Philadelphia in April 2007 to a group of Christian Scientists who had established a fund for Christian Science practitioners.

In June 2007 we went first to Vence, France, where we visited Fred Spotts. Then we spent another week in a nearby mountain town, St. Jennet, and we visited daily with Fred. We also spent a day with Anne-Marie Schweighofer, seeing her in her home and reliving memories of family and friends. And then we flew to Copenhagen and spent two separate weekends with the Lansings. Kathie and I went to Berlin between those two weekends. We toured Potsdam and Berlin with Joachim and Renate Trapp and also saw old friends Ellen and Michael Bohle, who gave us a great tour of reconstructed East Berlin as well as the Holocaust Memorial.

* * * *

Editor's note: Dick Nenneman died suddenly on December 27, 2007, in Concord, Massachusetts. In addition to notices and obituaries in *The Boston Globe* and local newspapers, *The Christian Science Monitor* ran the following appreciation on December 31, 2007:

AN APPRECIATION

The former editor in chief of The Christian Science Monitor had a high-octane intellect and love of world affairs.

By David T. Cook

When Richard A. Nenneman first joined this newspaper as its business editor in 1965, he made quite an impression on his staff. He usually arrived well after the worker bees, and he instructed them not to talk to him on mornings when he wrote. Then, he thumbed through The Wall Street Journal, put his feet on the desk, pondered, and in roughly an hour, pounded out an insightful column on his portable Smith Corona electric typewriter.

This, from a man with no prior professional journalism experience, but with a high-octane intellect. His writing won him top awards in business journalism and access to key contacts on Wall Street and in Washington. He later became the managing editor of The Christian Science Monitor, and then its editor in chief. Mr. Nenneman died on Dec. 27.

The Monitor was the much-loved center but not the exclusive focus of his varied professional life. The tall and refined Harvard graduate came to the paper after service as a U.S. Army counter intelligence operative in Germany and an early career in banking. He left in 1974 to return to the business world, rising to become senior vice president of Girard Bank in Philadelphia. In 1983, he rejoined the paper for a decade in leadership positions.

He had a quiet demeanor that masked a wry sense of humor and a keen interest in mentoring young staffers, whom he often invited to the home he shared with his wife, Katherine, and their three daughters Ann, Kate, and Mary.

Congressman Lamar Smith (R) of Texas spent time as a young reporter working for Nenneman. "He taught by example and you never wanted to disappoint him," Representative Smith said.

Regardless of the personal or professional challenges he faced, Nenneman seemed always engaged in the life of the mind. "Whenever I saw him, I recall him mentioning some book he had been reading usually something hefty, deep, and ponderous with great enthusiasm," said Jeremy Cattani, who worked with Nenneman when he oversaw the Monitor's TV operations.

Nenneman turned his trademark candor and well-honed analytical powers on the Monitor's own business challenges in ways that sometimes made him a controversial figure among newsroom colleagues. He oversaw a challenging period in which the paper expanded into television and radio, and senior editors resigned. Looking back, he observed in a 2001 interview with the Harvard Crimson, "Print [media] has to adjust to the new world in which it is primarily interpretive and investigative."

In 1993, soon after the Monitor's expansive broadcast activities were shuttered, Nenneman retired.

"The Monitor's mission was very much in Dick's heart," said Richard Bergenheim, the Monitor's current editor. "His interest and desire to contribute to the Monitor's progress and its impact on the world never diminished."

Nenneman's idea of retirement included researching and writing a biography, "Persistent Pilgrim," about Mary Baker Eddy, the founder of Christian Science and this newspaper. It followed on other book projects, including "The New Birth of Christianity: Why Religion Persists in a Scientific Age," which he authored, and "How Peace Came to the World," a collection of Monitor essays, which he co-edited with former Monitor editor Earl Foell.

This fall, Nenneman was still "booking" it. Earlier this month he completed editing and writing the preface for "In the Nation's Service," a compendium of essays by his fellow members of the 1951 Harvard class on their military and public service.

And he took special joy in his work for the Executive Service Corp., providing pro bono consulting to nonprofit organizations including the National Braille Press.

His well-lived life brings to mind words he spoke while moderating a panel discussion of Monitor journalists in 1984. "No matter how comfortable each of us may be at home," Nenneman said, "the demands of authentic love should impel us all to enlarge our tents, to include that sense of family that knows no division of time or place."

By David Cook. Reproduced with permission from the December 31, 2007, issue of The Christian Science Monitor (www.csmonitor.com). ©2007 The Christian Science Monitor. All rights reserved.

BIBLIOGRAPHY

Abelard	Sic et Non (Yes and No)
Karen Armstrong	Islam
Allan Bloom	The Closing of the American Mind
Dietrich Bonhoeffer	A Testament to Freedom: The Essential Writings of Dietrich Bonhoeffer
	Letters and Papers from Prison
	Life Together
	The Cost of Discipleship
Marcus Borg	Meeting Jesus Again for the First Time
Marcus Borg and N. T. Wright	The Meaning of Jesus
Thomas Cahill	Desire of the Everlasting Hills
James Carroll	The Sword of Constantine
Mary Ellen Chase	The Prophets for the Common Reader
David Chidester	Christianity, A Global History
James Freeman Clarke	Ten Great Religions
John Dominic Crossan	The Birth of Christianity
John P. Dourley	Jung, Tillich, and Aspects of Western Christian Development
Mary Baker Eddy	Miscellaneous Writings
	Science and Health with Key to the Scriptures

Ralph Waldo Emerson	Essays, Self Reliance
	The American Scholar
	The Over-Soul
Northrop Frye	The Great Code
Gary Gunderson	Deeply Women Roots
Abraham Heschel	God in Search of Man
Hermann Hesse	The Glass Bead Game
Harry Hoehler	Christian Responses to the World's Faith
William James	A Pluralistic Universe
	The Varieties of Religious Experience
Richard Nenneman	The New Birth of Christianity: Why Religion Persists In A Scientific Age
	Persistent Pilgrim: The Life of Mary Baker Eddy
Richard Niebuhr	The Responsible Self: An Essay in Christian Moral Philosophy
Henri Nouwen	The Only Necessary Thing: Living a Prayerful Life
Robert Richardson	Emerson: The Mind of Fire
Ronald Rolheiser	The Holy Longing: The Search for a Christian Spirituality
Albert Schweitzer	The Quest for the Historical Jesus

Paul Tillich	A History of Christian Thought
David Weissbard	Ten Commandments (a manuscript)
A.N. Wilson	God's Funeral